World War I
Almanac

World War I
Almanac

Tom Pendergast
and Sara Pendergast

Christine Slovey, Editor

GALE GROUP

THOMSON LEARNING

Detroit • New York • San Diego • San Francisco
Boston • New Haven, Conn. • Waterville, Maine
London • Munich

World War I: Almanac

Tom Pendergast
Sara Pendergast

Staff

Christine Slovey, *U•X•L Senior Editor*
Elizabeth Shaw Grunow, *U•X•L Contributing Editor*
Carol DeKane Nagel, *U•X•L Managing Editor*
Tom Romig, *U•X•L Publisher*

Shalice Shah-Caldwell, *Permissions Associate (Pictures)*
Robyn Young, *Imaging and Multimedia Content Editor*
Pamela A. Reed, *Imaging Coordinator*

Rita Wimberly, *Senior Buyer*
Evi Seoud, *Assistant Manager, Composition Purchasing and Electronic Prepress*

Pamela A.E. Galbreath, *Senior Art Designer*
Jennifer Wahi, *Art Designer*

Linda Mahoney, LM Design, *Typesetting*

Cover Photos: Woman welder, reproduced courtesy of the Library of Congress; United States Army Signal Corps, reproduced by permission of AP/Wide World Photos; Celebrating the Armistice, reproduced by permission of the Corbis Corporation (Bellevue).

Library of Congress Cataloging-in-Publication Data

Pendergast, Tom.
    World War I almanac / Tom Pendergast, Sara Pendergast ; edited by Christine Slovey.
        p.cm.
    Includes bibliographical references (p.) and index.
    ISBN 0-7876-5476-0 (alk. paper)
    1. World War, 1914-1918. I. Title: World War One almanac. II. Title: World War 1 almanac. III. Pendergast, Sara. IV. Slovey, Christine. V. Title.
D521 .P37 2001

940.3—dc21   2001053012

Printed in the United States of America

10 9 8 7 6 5 4 3 2 1

Contents

**Memorial Day,
Brookwood, Surrey.**
*Reproduced by permission
of Archive Photos, Inc.*

Reader's Guide

World War I was truly one of the most tragic events of the twentieth century. The war began over a terrorist act in the provinces of the fading Austro-Hungarian Empire and could have been avoided if Germany, Russia, and France hadn't felt compelled to obey secret treaties they had signed years before. Those secret treaties turned a small conflict into one that involved every major country in Europe and eventually many other nations from around the world. In the course of just over four years of war, nearly ten million soldiers and civilians lost their lives; billions of dollars were spent on killing machines—guns, tanks, submarines—and the economies of most of the warring countries were severely disrupted; two great empires—the Austro-Hungarian Empire and the Ottoman Empire—collapsed in defeat.

At the end of this terrible conflict, little had changed. Ethnic conflicts in the Balkan region continued to pit neighbor against neighbor. Attempts to create an international organization that would ensure world peace collapsed when the United States withdrew its support. Germany, though defeated, remained at odds with its rivals, France and England,

and military leaders within Germany longed to avenge their defeat. Within twenty years of the end of World War I these simmering tensions sparked another war, World War II, which returned death and destruction to the continent of Europe and to battlefields all over the world.

Features

World War I: Almanac covers the war in twelve thematic chapters, each geared toward offering an understanding of a single element of the conflict, from the underlying causes of the war to the many battles fought on the various fronts to the anguished attempt to establish world peace at the war's end. More than 70 black-and-white photos and maps illustrate the text. Numerous sidebars highlight interesting individuals and fascinating facts. The volume also includes a glossary, a timeline, research and activities ideas, sources for further reading, and a subject index.

Related Reference Sources

World War I: Biographies (one volume) presents biographies of thirty men and women who were involved in World War I. Profiled are readily recognizable figures, such as U.S. president Woodrow Wilson and German leader Kaiser Wilhelm II, as well as lesser-known people like Jewish spy Sarah Aaronsohn and English nurse Edith Cavell.

World War I: Primary Sources (one volume) offers thirty-three full or excerpted documents from the World War I era. Included are Woodrow Wilson's "Fourteen Points" speech; excerpts from Ernest Hemingway's novel Farewell to Arms; poems from leading war poets such as Alan Seeger and Rupert Brooke; and the "Dual Alliance" secret treaty between Germany and Austria-Hungary. A sampling of propaganda posters and numerous first-person accounts from soldiers at the front are also present.

Dedication

To our children, Conrad and Louisa.

Special Thanks

We'd like to thank several people who have contributed to the creation of this book. We could ask for no better editor than Christine Slovey at U•X•L, who saw this book through most of its creation and always helped make our job easier. Dick Hetland—chair of the social studies department and teacher of twentieth-century American history at Snohomish High School in Snohomish, Washington—offered invaluable advice on how to shape the content of this book to fit the needs of students.

There are many others who contributed to this book without even knowing it. They are the historians and scholars who contributed their skills to writing books and articles on one of the most tragic events in human history. Their names can be found in the bibliographies of every chapter, and our debt to them is great.

Suggestions

We welcome any comments on the *World War I: Almanac*. Please write: Editors, *World War I: Almanac*, U•X•L, Gale Group, 27500 Drake Road, Farmington Hills, Michigan, 48331-3535; call toll-free: 800-877-4253; or fax to: 248-699-8097; or e-mail via www.galegroup.com.

Timeline

1871   German states unify after defeating France in 1870; the Franco-Prussian war is the source of some of the hatred between France and Germany

1872   The emperors of Germany, Austria-Hungary, and Russia pledge their friendship to each other in the League of the Three Emperors

1879   Germany and Austria-Hungary create the Dual Alliance

1904   Britain and France sign the Entente Cordiale, an agreement settling long-running arguments over colonial territories and promising future cooperation in military affairs

1908   Austria-Hungary annexes the provinces of Bosnia and Herzegovina, angering Serbia, which wanted to dominate the Balkan region

1914   **June 28** Austrian Archduke Franz Ferdinand is assassinated by Serbian nationalist Gavrilo Princip in Sarajevo

July 23 Austria-Hungary issues an ultimatum concerning the investigation of the assasination to Serbia; Serbia refused to comply with its terms

Police apprehending Gavrilo Princip after he assassinated Crown Prince Franz Ferdinand. *Reproduced by permission of the Corbis Corporation (Bellevue).*

German machine gun corps protecting the flank of advancing troops.
Reproduced by permission of Archive Photos, Inc.

July 28 Austria-Hungary declares war on Serbia

August 1 Germany declares war on Russia

August 3 Germany declares war on France; German troops enter Belgium

August 4 Great Britain declares war on Germany; Germany declares war on Belgium; United States declares its neutrality

August 6 Austria-Hungary declares war on Russia; Serbia declares war on Germany

August 10 Frances declares war on Austro-Hungary

Mid-August Russian forces defeat Germans in skirmishes in eastern Prussia

August 14 French and German troops clash in the Alsace-Lorraine region

August 16 Belgium surrenders its fortress at Liège

August 23 Battle of Mons pits Germans against French and British

August 25-31 Russia is defeated by Germany in the Battle of Tannenberg

August 26 French and British troops take the German colony of Togo

August 28 Naval Battle of Heligoland Bight in the North Sea

September 5 A German submarine scores its first kill, sinking the British cruiser *Pathfinder*

September 6-10 In the Battle of the Marne, the German advance into France is halted and Allied and German forces dig in to the trenches from which they will fight for the remainder of the war

October 29 The Ottoman Empire (Turkey) joins the Central Powers (Germany and Austria-Hungary)

October 29-November 22 First Battle of Ypres

November 1 Naval Battle of Colonel

November 3 Great Britain declares the North Sea a war zone and places mines in the water to destroy German shipping

November 6 France and Great Britain declare war on Turkey

November 7 Germans surrender the Chinese port of Tsingtao

December 20-March 10, 1915 First Battle of Champagne

1915 **January-February** Winter Battle of Masuria between Russia, Germany, and Austria-Hungary

January 24 Naval Battle of Dogger Bank

February 4 Germany declares a "war zone" around the British Isles, hoping to stop shipping to the island nation

February 9 British and French begin assault on Gallipoli in Turkey

March 11 Great Britain announces a blockade of German ports, hoping to starve the Germans of needed food and supplies

April 22 Poison gas is used for the first time in the Second Battle of Ypres

April 24 Turks begin massacre of Armenians

April 26 France, Russia, Italy, and Great Britain conclude the secret treaty of London

May 2 Germans begin an assault that drives Russia out of Poland

May 7 A German submarine sinks the British passenger liner *Lusitania,* killing 1,198 people, including 128 Americans. U.S. President Woodrow Wilson continues to proclaim American neutrality

May 23 Italy declares war on Austria-Hungary, honoring a secret treaty it had signed with the Allies (France, Great Britain, Russia, Belgium, and later the United States)

June 6 German naval commanders order German submarines to stop sinking passenger ships

June 9 U.S. president Wilson sends Germany a strong protest against Germany's use of submarine warfare

General Paul von Hindenburg, Kaiser Wilhelm II, and General Erich Ludendorff.
Reproduced by permission of the Corbis Corporation (Bellevue).

French soldier falling after being shot near Verdun.
Reproduced by permission of the Corbis Corporation (Bellevue).

June 23 Italy begins fighting near Isonzo in the first of what will be twelve battles near this small town

July 9 German forces surrender colony of German Southwest Africa

September 1 Germany ends unrestricted submarine warfare, hoping to keep the United States from siding with the Allies

September 6 Bulgaria joins the Central Powers, attacks Serbia

September 25 Battle of Loos

October 6 Serbia is invaded by the Central Powers

October 15 Great Britain declares war on Bulgaria

October 23 Allied troops are evacuated from Gallipoli after being defeated by Turkish forces

December 3 Joseph "Papa" Joffre is named commander-in-chief of French forces

December 8 Naval Battle of the Falkland Islands

December 17 Douglas Haig is named commander in chief of British forces, replacing John Haig

1916 **January 11** Russia begins attack on Turkish forces in the Caucasus region

February 21-December 18 The Battle of Verdun, in which German forces attack French fortresses near the town of Verdun; this is the longest single battle of the war

February 28 German forces in Cameroon surrender

May 31 Naval Battle of Jutland

April 24 The Easter Rebellion for Irish independence is crushed by British troops

June 4-September 30 Brusilov offensive, in which Russians attack Austro-Hungarian and German forces

June 1-November 13 Battle of the Somme between Germans and Allies; the British use tanks for the first time in this battle on September 15

August 27 Romania enters the war on the side of the Allies

August 27 Italy declares war on Germany

August 29 Generals Paul von Hindenburg and Erich Ludendorff take charge of the German military

September-November British forces march up Tigres-Euphrates valley, hoping to take Baghdad, but are defeated at Kut on April 29, 1917

November 7 Woodrow Wilson is reelected as President of the United States; he campaigns on the pledge to keep the United States out of war

December 7 David Lloyd George becomes British Prime Minister

1917   **February 1** Germans renew unrestricted submarine warfare

February 3 The United States breaks off diplomatic relations with Germany

February 23 Germans begin their withdrawal to the Hindenburg Line, a defensive position to the rear of the present front

March 12 First revolution in Russia; Czar Nicholas II abdicates on March 15

April 6 The United States declares war on Germany

April 16 Battle of the Aisne (also known as the Neville offensive) signals new French strategy, but the offensive fails within two weeks

April 16 220,000 German workers stage peaceful strike protesting the war

June 25 First American troops arrive in France

July 1-November 10   Third Battle of Ypres, or Passchendaele

October 24 Italians defeated by combined German and Austrian forces at Caporetto

November 4 British forces arrive in Italy

November 7 Bolshevik forces seize power in Russia

November 20 British use tanks effectively in Battle of Cambrai

Child in a refugee camp in Salonika, Greece.
Reproduced by permission of Archive Photos, Inc.

British tank *Winston's Folly* going over a trench.
Reproduced by permission of the Corbis Corporation (Bellevue).

December 2 Fighting ends on Eastern Front

December 7 United States declares war on Austria-Hungary

December 15 Germans and Russians sign armistice; peace talks start a week later at Brest-Litovsk

1918   **January 8** U.S. President Woodrow Wilson delivers "Fourteen Points" address before Congress

April 28 Gavrilo Princip dies in the Theresienstadt prison in Austria

March 3 Treaty of Brest-Litovsk signed between Germany and Russia

March 21 Germans break through Allied front near the Somme, beginning their "Spring Offensives"

March 23-April 9 Germans shell the city of Paris

May 7 Treaty of Bucharest ends fighting between Romania and Central Powers

July 15-18 Second Battle of the Marne, in which German forces begin to retreat

July 18-August 15 Allied Aisne-Marne offensive

August 8 Known as the "blackest day" for the German army, which was defeated in several key fights on this day and fell into a headlong retreat

September 12-16 American offensive at Saint-Mihiel

September 14 Allies begin assault on Germans and Austro-Hungarians along the Salonika Front in Greece

September 25-27 Allies launch the Meuse-Argonne Offensive, the last major attack of the war and one in which American troops see significant action

September 29 Bulgaria becomes the first of the Central Powers to surrender

October 20 Germany abandons submarine warfare

October 29 German sailors mutiny against their commanders

October 20 Turkey makes peace with the Allies

November 3 Austria-Hungary makes peace with the Allies

November 9 Kaiser Wilhelm II abdicates his throne; elected German officials declare the existence of the German Republic

November 11 Germany signs armistice with the Allies

November 21 German navy surrenders to the British

1919   **January 4** Peace conference begins in Paris

       June 28 Treaty of Versailles signed

       November 19 U.S. Senate refuses to ratify Treaty of Versailles

1921   **July 2** U.S. President Warren Harding signs a congressional joint resolution officially ending the war with Germany

Happy Parisians during a celebration of the end of World War I. *Reproduced by permission of Archive Photos, Inc.*

Words to Know

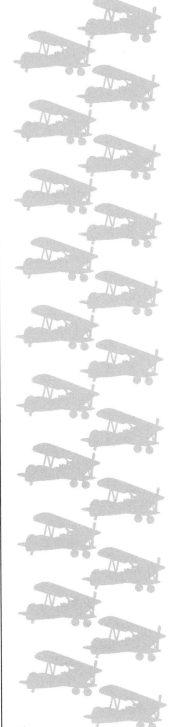

Allies: The nations who joined together to fight the Central Powers during World War I; they included France, Great Britain, Russia, Belgium, Italy, the United States, and several smaller countries.

Armistice: A temporary stop in fighting, or truce.

Artillery: Large-caliber weapons such as cannons and missile launchers that are capable of firing shells from a long distance.

Attrition: The gradual reduction in the strength of an army due to men being killed in battle.

Bolsheviks: A group of radical Russian activists who led the 1917 revolution in that country.

Bond: A certificate of debt issued by a government that promises repayment at a later date, plus interest; bonds were sold to raise money to support the war effort.

Campaign: A series of military operations undertaken to achieve a larger goal in war; a campaign will often consist of a number of battles.

Casualty: A soldier injured, killed, captured, or missing in the course of a battle; military strategists counted casualties as a way of assessing the damage done in a battle or campaign.

Cavalry: A military body that uses horses to move about the field of battle; after World War I, which saw the end of the use of horses in warfare, cavalry was used to refer to a mobile army force that used vehicles.

Central Powers: The nations who joined together to fight the Allies during World War I; they included Germany, the Austro-Hungarian Empire, the Ottoman Empire (Turkey), and several smaller nations.

Chancellor: The leader of the German parliament, similar to a British prime minister.

Combatant: One who participates in a fight.

Conscription: Forced enrollment in the armed forces; often referred to as the draft.

Convoy: A group of ships sailing together in order to provide protection from submarine attacks.

Diplomacy: The practice of conducting international relations, including making treaties and alliances.

Dreadnought: A large, heavily armored war ship.

Empire: A political unit consisting of several or many territories governed by a single supreme authority; before World War I, several of the combatant countries—including the Ottoman Empire, France, the United Kingdom, and the Austro-Hungarian Empire—were considered empires because they ruled distant colonies from their capitol.

Entente Cordiale: French for "friendly understanding," this 1904 agreement between Britain and France promised cooperation in military affairs.

Exile: Enforced removal from one's native country.

Fascism: A system of government in which all authority—military, economic, and governmental—is held in the hands of a single ruler.

Flank: The side of a military formation; one army "flanked" another by attacking its side, where it was weakest.

Fleet: A group of warships under a single command.

Front: The front line of a combat force in battle; the point at which two armies meet.

Genocide: The organized extermination of an entire national, racial, political, or ethnic group.

Imperial: Having the characteristics of an empire.

Infantry: Foot soldiers; the majority of soldiers in an army, these soldiers are trained to fight and advance on foot.

Internationalism: The political belief that the world would be better off if all countries worked together to solve their problems; this was the opposite of "isolationism."

Isolationism: An American political viewpoint that held that Americans should avoid becoming involved, or "entangled," in European problems.

Matériel: Military equipment and supplies.

Mobilization: The act of organizing military forces in preparation for war.

Mortar: A portable cannon used to fire explosive shells at the enemy over a fairly short distance.

Mutiny: Open rebellion against authority.

Nationalism: Fervent commitment to one's nation.

Neutrality: An official government policy which declares that the country in question will not take sides in a war.

No-Man's-Land: The area between two armies, especially two armies fighting in trench warfare; No-Man's-Land could be as narrow as a hundred feet or as wide as a half a mile.

Parapet: An earthen embankment protecting soldiers from enemy fire.

Pogrom: An organized massacre or persecution of a minority group, often used to refer to the persecution of Jewish people.

Reformer: One who is committed to improving conditions, usually in politics or civic life.

Reparations: Cash payments for damages done during wartime.

Salient: A military term that describes a position held by one army that juts or bulges forward into the line of the other army. A military front without a salient is a straight line; one with a salient may have a variety of curvy shapes.

Shell-shock: A form of mental distress caused by coming under fire in battle.

Shrapnel: Fragments from an explosive shell.

Siege: A blockade placed around a town or armed fortress in order to defeat those inside it.

Sniper: A skilled marksman whose job is to shoot enemy soldiers from a concealed position.

Theater: A broad area in which military operations are conducted.

Treaty: A formal agreement between two countries.

Research and Activity Ideas

The following ideas and projects might be used to supplement your classroom work on understanding the great conflict that was World War I:

Build a Model: Build a model that illustrates your understanding of World War I. You might build a scale model of a battlefield that shows the arrangement of trenches, machine gun nests, and artillery. You could create a moveable diorama of a battle at sea, such as the Battle of Jutland, and move the ships around to show how the conflict unfolded. Or you could construct scale models of several different pieces of equipment, such as an artillery piece or a gas mask.

Maps: Maps are wonderful tools to demonstrate how opposing forces faced each other on a battlefield; the best maps can even show how events changed over time. Using your understanding of a particular single battle or of a series of battles on one of the important fronts of the war, create a map that shows how—and if you're really good, why—the battle turned out like it did.

Poetry: World War I is known for its great poets. Educated men like Wilfred Owen, Alan Seeger, and Siegfried Sassoon all recorded their reactions to war in some of the most memorable poems in the English language. Using what you know about World War I, write a poem that captures an element of warfare that is striking to you. You might write it in the "old fashioned" language of the time or in your own language. For an interesting challenge, try expressing the same ideas in the language of the past and the present.

What If . . . ?: Historians love to ponder how the world would have turned out if things happened differently than they really did. What would have happened, for example, if Abraham Lincoln wasn't assassinated near the end of the American Civil War, or if the Americans didn't drop the atomic bomb on Japan at the end of World War II? There are many such questions you might ask about World War I as well. Pick an important moment in World War I and write a short paper exploring what might have happened had things turned out differently. For example, what if . . . the Russians had succeeded in their early attacks against the German army, or Germany had defeated the French at Verdun?

The Art of War: You are an important artist who has been assigned by your government to travel to the front to record your impressions of the war. What do you paint? Scenes of battle and violence, or the quiet life of soldiers waiting for the call to combat? And how do you paint it? Do you use harsh images and gory detail to show war's horror, or do you owe it to your country to paint scenes that glorify the actions of our country's soldiers? Paint a picture or create a series of drawings that show how you would portray the war. For a challenge, write a statement justifying why you decided to paint the way you did.

Book Report: There are a variety of books, both fiction and nonfiction, that discuss in great detail many aspects of World War I. Work with your librarian to find a book about World War I that interests you. Then prepare a book report for your classmates that helps them understand the new perspective that the book has given you. Talk with your teacher about how to construct an effective book report.

World War I on the World Wide Web: The Internet has proven to be a wonderful place for historians and war buffs to display the images and ideas relating to World War I. In fact, there are dozens and dozens of Web sites relating to World War I. Create a student's guide to World War I on the Web, selecting those sites that you think are most worthwhile and explaining to your fellow students what they can expect to learn from the five best Web sites. Or, create your own Web site about a World War I topic that interests you, with links to other related Web sites.

Biographies: Sometimes an individual life provides the best way of understanding the impact of an event like World War I. Choose an individual that you are interested in and write a biographical essay that explores how the war affected his or her life. Consult with your teacher about how to construct the essay and how many sources you might want to consult.

Museum Review: You may be lucky enough to live close to a museum that has an exhibit concerning World War I. Write a review of the exhibit. You might discuss the kinds of items that the museum curator used to tell the story of World War I, or what it was like to see firsthand such things as gas masks, machine guns, and models of life in the trenches.

World War I
Almanac

Buildup to War

1

On June 28, 1914, in the streets of Sarajevo, a young Bosnian terrorist named Gavrilo Princip assassinated Archduke Franz Ferdinand, the heir to the throne of the Austro-Hungarian Empire. This single event triggered a chain reaction that slowly drew every major European nation and many other nations around the world into the bloodiest war yet known to humanity, a war now known as World War I. But World War I was not caused by a single gunshot. It arose out of tensions that had gripped Europe for nearly fifty years. To understand how and why the war began, one must first understand the conditions in Europe before the war.

Though it is known as World War I, the conflict that shook the world from 1914 to 1918 had its roots in a European conflict. When it began, the Great War, as it was first known, pitted the Dual Alliance of Germany and Austria-Hungary against the Triple Entente of France, Russia, and Great Britain in a dispute over Serbian interference in Austro-Hungarian affairs. (Upon entering into war the opposing sides are known in this work as the Central Powers and the Allies, respectively.) The most important and bloody battles of the war were fought

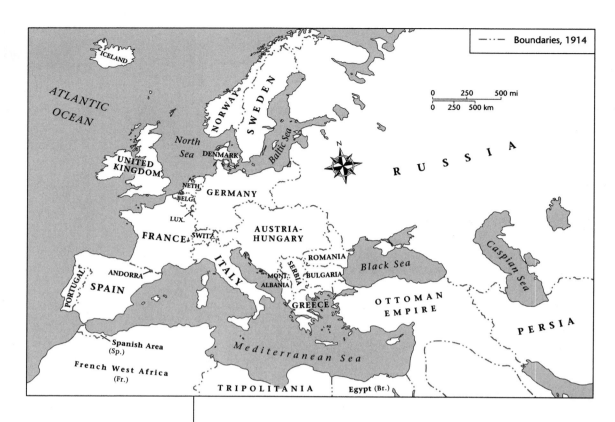

Boundaries, 1914

ATLANTIC OCEAN

ICELAND

NORWAY

SWEDEN

North Sea

DENMARK

Baltic Sea

RUSSIA

UNITED KINGDOM

NETH.

BELG.

GERMANY

LUX.

FRANCE

SWITZ.

AUSTRIA-HUNGARY

ROMANIA

Black Sea

Caspian Sea

PORTUGAL

ANDORRA

SPAIN

ITALY

MONT.

SERBIA

ALBANIA

BULGARIA

GREECE

OTTOMAN EMPIRE

PERSIA

Spanish Area (Sp.)

French West Africa (Fr.)

Mediterranean Sea

TRIPOLITANIA

Egypt (Br.)

0   250   500 mi
0   250   500 km

Europe in 1914, prior to the onset of World War I.
Reproduced by permission of The Gale Group.

on European soil. But the war also spread to involve the far-flung colonies and allies of the larger warring empires.

The Shape of Europe

Western Europe at the dawn of World War I looked much as it does today, with France and Germany the dominant geographic and economic powers on the Continent. It had not always been this way. In fact, a hundred years earlier there had been no German nation, but rather a scattering of independent Germanic states. Beginning in the 1860s the state of Prussia, led by Otto von Bismarck (1815–1898), began to conquer the other Germanic states in a series of short wars. Prussia defeated Denmark in 1863 and Austria in 1865, proving itself the dominant power in Europe—except for France. Finally, in 1870, Prussia and its allied German states attacked France. To the surprise of many observers, Prussia and its allies defeated the French, and by doing so they changed the political landscape of Europe.

Following the Franco-Prussian War, in January 1871 the Germans unified their twenty-six independent states into the German Empire. They named Prussian King Wilhelm I (1797–1888) their emperor, or kaiser, and Bismarck became the chancellor, the German equivalent of a prime minister. One of the first acts of the German Empire was to penalize France for its recent defeat in war. The Germans claimed the French provinces of Alsace and Lorraine for their own and forced the French to pay reparations (cash payments for damages done during wartime). These penalties were perceived as a grave insult by the French and ensured that the two countries would remain enemies for years to come.

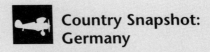

Country Snapshot: Germany

- Total population (1913): 66.9 million
- Industrial Potential (1913; Britain in 1900 = 100): 137.7*
- Share of World Manufacturing Output (1913; as percentage of whole): 14.8 percent
- Military and Naval Personnel (1914): 891,000
- Warship Tonnage (1914): 1,305,000**

(Paul Kennedy, The Rise and Fall of the Great Powers *[New York: Random House, 1987], p. 199.)*

* *This is a relative measure of the strengths of the various economies.*

** *This is a measure of the number of tons of water displaced by a nation's warships.*

German Alliances

The Franco-Prussian War established Germany as a major power in Europe, but the German Empire was far from strong enough to succeed on its own. To the east of Germany lay Russia, a vast country with a huge population. Hoping to ensure that it would not have to battle both France and Russia at the same time, Germany initially sought friendship with the Russians. In 1872 Bismarck engineered an agreement known as the League of the Three Emperors, in which the emperors of Germany, Austria-Hungary, and Russia pledged their friendship to each other. That alliance was renewed and made more lasting with the Reinsurance Treaty of 1887, in which Germany and Russia pledged not to go to war with one another. But friendship with Russia was not to last. Kaiser Wilhelm I died in 1888, and his grandson, Wilhelm II, took the throne; Bismarck, architect of the peace with Russia, soon left office. Relations between German and Russian leaders quickly broke down, and before long Russia entered into a more secure alliance with Germany's enemy, France.

Germany's strongest alliance was with Austria-Hungary, its neighbor to the south. Austria-Hungary was the oldest of the European monarchies, and it was ruled by the longest-serving head of state, the Emperor Franz Josef I. Franz Josef I had taken the throne in 1848; by 1914, the aging Franz Josef had been in power for sixty-six years. The Austro-Hungarian Empire consisted of two separate states that shared a single emperor and followed a single military and foreign policy. The

Austrian half of the partnership had its capital in Vienna, and the Hungarian half-claimed Budapest as its capital. The Hungarian half of the empire was split into a variety of ethnic groups: Half of its inhabitants were Magyars (ethnic Hungarians), but there were significant minorities of Romanians, Germans, Slovaks, Croatians, and Serbs. These ethnic divisions would eventually lead to the breakup of the empire.

Germany first allied itself with Austria-Hungary in the League of the Three Emperors (1872). In 1879, however, the leaders of Germany and Austria-Hungary created the Dual Alliance, in which the two countries agreed to support each other in any military conflict. When Kaiser Wilhelm II took power in 1888 and ended the German friendship with Russia, he strengthened German ties with Austria. Wilhelm II felt that he could dominate the partnership with Austria-Hungary. Little did he know that this weaker partner would soon draw Germany into a war that it might otherwise have avoided.

Franz Josef I, Emperor of Austria and King of Hungary. *Reproduced by permission of Archive Photos, Inc.*

France and Russia

Despite its defeat by the Germans in 1870, France was still a powerful nation. Following the Franco-Prussian War, the French quickly developed one of the strongest economies in Europe; they also built one of the strongest armies in the world. Yet they could not help but fear the growing power of Germany, especially as it secured an alliance with Austria-Hungary that extended German power from the North Sea to the Baltic Sea. As Russia slipped from the German embrace in the 1890s, France sought to strengthen ties with the Russians.

France and Russia were very different countries. A republic since the fall of Napoléon III in 1870, France had the most representative government on the Continent. The

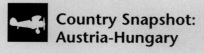

Country Snapshot: Austria-Hungary

- Total population (1913): 52.1 million

- Industrial Potential (1913; Britain in 1900 = 100): 40.7*

- Share of World Manufacturing Output (1913; as percentage of whole): 4.4 percent

- Military and Naval Personnel (1914): 444,000

- Warship Tonnage (1914): 372,000**

(Paul Kennedy, The Rise and Fall of the Great Powers *[New York: Random House, 1987], p. 199.)*

* This is a relative measure of the strengths of the various economies.

**This is a measure of the number of tons of water displaced by a nation's warships.

French people elected a two-house legislature, which selected the country's president; the president in turn selected a prime minister. Russia, on the other hand, had one of the least representative and most authoritarian governments. Russia was led after 1894 by Czar Nicholas II. (Czar, also spelled *tsar,* is a Russian term for emperor; the czar was also known as "Emperor and Autocrat of all Russias.") Power in Russia was shared by the czar and an elected parliament, but it was not shared equally: The czar had full control over military affairs. Despite their differences, both France and Russia wished to contain the power of Great Britain's colonial empire and defend themselves against the growing strength of the Dual Alliance.

By 1894 France and Russia had entered into an alliance of their own. They agreed to share military plans and to protect each other in case of war. France loaned Russia money to help it construct a railroad spanning the vast Russian countryside. Both countries agreed that they needed to protect the Slavic peoples living to the east of the Austro-Hungarian border. And both countries were concerned about the power of the world's greatest empire, the British Empire.

The British Empire

Lying just off the continent of Europe was one of the most powerful nations in the world, Great Britain. What made Great Britain so powerful? As the first nation in the world to experience the industrial revolution, Britain had a powerful economy. It had many factories and its banking system was strong. More importantly, Britain had colonies and territories scattered throughout the world, including India, Australia,

New Zealand, Canada, and portions of Africa and the Caribbean. Legend had it that "the sun never set on the British Empire." These colonies and territories provided markets for British goods and raw material for British factories. In order to protect its interests around the world, Britain had built the world's most powerful navy.

The growing strength of Germany, France, and Russia concerned Great Britain. These countries were also eager to build their empires by establishing colonies and trading relationships in other parts of the world. Russia was interested in gaining influence in Afghanistan; France wanted to extend its influence in Africa; and Germany's Kaiser Wilhelm II launched a plan for expansion he called *welt-politik,* or world scheme. By the turn of the century, Germany had colonies in China, Western Samoa, and Africa. Britain worried that the race for empire would bring on a war. It needed to find an ally among the European powers. But which one?

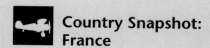

Country Snapshot: France

- Total population (1913): 39.7 million
- Industrial Potential (1913; Britain in 1900 = 100): 57.3*
- Share of World Manufacturing Output (1913; as percentage of whole): 6.1 percent
- Military and Naval Personnel (1914): 910,000
- Warship Tonnage (1914): 900,000**

(Paul Kennedy, The Rise and Fall of the Great Powers [New York: Random House, 1987], p. 199.)

*   This is a relative measure of the strengths of the various economies.

** This is a measure of the number of tons of water displaced by a nation's warships.

In the end, Britain allied itself with France and Russia. The reasons were many: Britain and France had a long history of cultural ties; Britain stood to gain the most by avoiding conflict with Russia and France; and Britain wanted to contain German expansion. In 1904 Britain and France signed the Entente Cordiale (an entente is an understanding), an agreement settling long-running arguments over colonial territories and promising future cooperation in military affairs. The Entente Cordiale was tested in 1905 and 1906 when France and Germany clashed over the African country of Morocco. Britain supported France in the conflict, thus ending German influence in Morocco. In 1907 Russia and Great Britain agreed to settle their differences in Afghanistan, Persia, and the Black Sea. Britain now joined with France and Russia in what was called the Triple Entente.

Kaiser Wilhelm II. *Reproduced by permission of Archive Photos, Inc.*

Booming Economies

The alliances and ententes that the major European powers entered into were designed to offer protection and stability. Germany had enemies on the west and east, but it knew it could rely on Austria-Hungary in case of war. France and Russia felt that together they could contain what they saw as Germany's desire to dominate Europe. Britain felt that it could best retain its empire with the help of France and Russia. The alliances offered a sense of peace, but they did not discourage competition between the countries. In the years leading up to World War I, each of the major combatant countries grew dramatically, both in population and in economic strength. As they grew, and watched each other grow, each country became wary of the other's power.

Though Britain had industrialized first (in the middle to late eighteenth century), by 1900 the most vibrant economy in Europe belonged to Germany. According to Stewart Ross, author of *Causes and Consequences of World War I,* "Between 1870 and 1914 Germany's coal production soared 800 percent to rival Britain's. By the outbreak of war, Germany was producing as much iron as Britain and twice as much steel. Its electricity output matched that of Britain, France, and Italy combined, while its electrical and chemical industries led the world." Germany's share of world manufacturing grew from 8.5 percent in 1880 to 14.8 percent in 1913; during the same period Britain's share fell from 22.9 percent to 13.6 percent, according to P. M. Kennedy in *The Rise and Fall of the Great Powers: Economic Change and Military Conflict from 1500 to 2000.*

Germany was not the only country growing quickly. France was also industrializing rapidly, and it shared its abundant capital with Russia, which grew to overtake France in the production of coal, iron, and steel. Perhaps even more than

France, Russia posed a threat to Germany. Its population was more than twice Germany's, and with French financial support, it seemed that Russia might soon threaten Germany's economic dominance. Across the seas lay yet another economic giant, the United States. Its growing production in the closing years of the nineteenth century promised that it would soon become the world's largest economy. Because the United States had no formal alliances with the European powers, it was free to supply war material to any country it liked.

Building Modern Armies

As the economic power of the countries grew, so too did their military power. But the military power of the combatant countries did not grow evenly. In fact, in the years leading up to the war, Germany fell behind Russia, France, and Britain in its ability to wage war (as measured by the number of men, ships, and guns it had available for the war effort). The story can largely be told in numbers.

Military thinkers at the turn of the twentieth century generally believed that victory in battle would go to the army that put the most soldiers into the field the quickest. Thus they placed a premium on having large standing armies and on having huge numbers of trained men ready to be called up for service. The Russians, with their large population, naturally had the largest army. Their peacetime strength (the number of soldiers in active service ready for battle) stood at 1,445,000 in 1914; they were capable of increasing this force to 3,400,000 in case of war, according to statistics quoted by Niall Ferguson in *The Pity of War*. France followed Russia in peacetime strength, with 827,000 soldiers, a force it could increase to 1,800,000 in wartime. With their allies—Belgium,

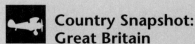

Country Snapshot: Great Britain

- Total population (1913): 45.6 million

- Industrial Potential (1913; Britain in 1900 = 100): 127.2*

- Share of World Manufacturing Output (1913; as percentage of whole): 13.6 percent

- Military and Naval Personnel (1914): 532,000

- Warship Tonnage (1914): 2,714,000**

(Paul Kennedy, The Rise and Fall of the Great Powers *[New York: Random House, 1987], p. 199.)*

* *This is a relative measure of the strengths of the various economies.*

** *This is a measure of the number of tons of water displaced by a nation's warships.*

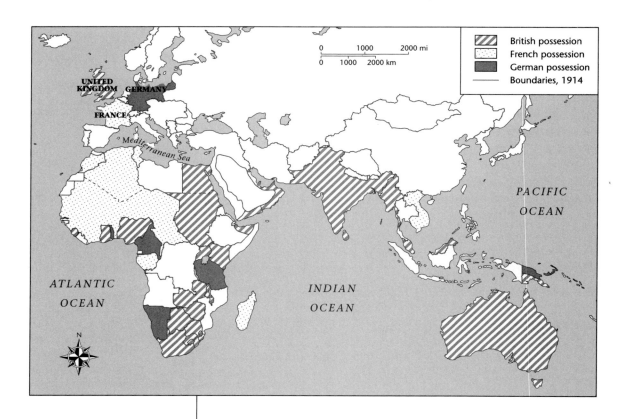

no

British possession
French possession
German possession
Boundaries, 1914

UNITED
KINGDOM   GERMANY
FRANCE

Mediterranean Sea

PACIFIC
OCEAN

ATLANTIC
OCEAN

INDIAN
OCEAN

N

European possessions around the world in 1914, prior to onset of World War I. *Reproduced by permission of The Gale Group.*

Serbia, and Montenegro—the Entente powers had a total peacetime army of 2,622,000 men and a total wartime strength of 5,726,000. Both the Russian and French armies relied on conscription, or required service in the armed forces. The British resisted calls for peacetime conscription and thus had a much smaller army.

German military leaders feared the huge and growing armies of France and Russia and bolstered their own army's strength accordingly. Military service laws passed in Germany in 1912 and 1913 increased the strength of the German army dramatically. By 1914, according to statistics cited by Ferguson, the German military had a peacetime strength of 761,000 men and was capable of increasing its wartime strength to 2,147,000. Austria-Hungary boasted a peacetime strength of 478,000 and could expand its army to a wartime strength of 1,338,000. Together, the Dual Alliance powers could count on a wartime army of 3,485,000 men—over 2 million men less than the Entente powers.

The Entente powers also had a significant advantage at sea, thanks to Britain's navy, which was known as the greatest in the world. In 1914, Britain boasted 209,000 naval personnel and 29 large naval vessels. Russia and France contributed 54,000 and 68,000 men and 4 and 10 large naval vessels, respectively. In total, the Entente countries had 331,000 men and 43 large naval vessels. German strategists had long feared British dominance on the seas. Their biggest fear was that a powerful British navy could blockade the import of food and supplies to Germany in case of war. Kaiser Wilhelm II wanted desperately to develop a world-class navy, and he poured money into the effort. Still, by 1914 Germany had just 79,000 naval personnel supporting 17 large naval vessels. Combined with Austria's meager navy—16,000 men and 3 large naval vessels—the Central Powers had only 95,000 men and 20 large naval vessels. Thus the Entente powers had three times as many men and twice as many ships at the beginning of the war. It was an advantage that would, in the end, prove impossible to overcome.

Battleships lined up for the king's review of the British fleet. *Reproduced by permission of Archive Photos, Inc.*

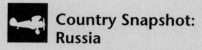

Country Snapshot: Russia

- Total population (1913): 175.1 million

- Industrial Potential (1913; Britain in 1900 = 100): 76.6*

- Share of World Manufacturing Output (1913; as percentage of whole): 8.2 percent

- Military and Naval Personnel (1914): 1,352,000

- Warship Tonnage (1914): 679,000**

(Paul Kennedy, The Rise and Fall of the Great Powers *[New York: Random House, 1987], p. 199.)*

* *This is a relative measure of the strengths of the various economies.*

***This is a measure of the number of tons of water displaced by a nation's warships.*

The numbers of men capable of fighting for the warring nations were important, but there were other factors to consider. Though Germany had fewer men than its enemies, German military strategists believed that they possessed a real lead in mobilization (the process of bringing an army to the field of battle). To mobilize well was to quickly bring soldiers, guns, and supplies to the front, and at this the Germans were prepared to excel. They had the most developed railway system on the Continent, and their general staff (bureaucrats in charge of war planning) had developed detailed plans for speeding troops to key positions. The Germans felt that in this area they were unrivaled in Europe. With its booming industrial capacity, Germany also had slight advantages in the number and quality of its weapons. Russia, for all its numbers, was known for mobilizing slowly and for having inferior weaponry. These failures would cost the Russians thousands of lives.

Steps on the Road to War

The mere existence of interlocking alliances and growing armies was not enough to drag Europe into war. In fact, despite popular fears in each of the eventual warring nations that the enemy was priming for attack, each country had good reasons to avoid war. In the first decade of the century, antiwar socialist political parties were slowly gaining power in France, Austria, Britain, Russia, and especially Germany. According to Ferguson, these parties were growing in strength because every country in Europe was extending the vote to more of its citizens. The number of votes going to antiwar socialist parties reached 25.4 percent in Austria in 1911, 16.8 percent in France in 1914, and 34.8 percent in Germany in 1912. These figures indicate that substantial minorities of citizens supported candidates who wanted to avoid European wars. Most businessmen too preferred to avoid war. Despite growing popular opinion against war, a series of diplomatic clashes brought war ever closer.

In 1905 the French sought to increase their influence in North Africa by declaring Morocco a French colony. Germany protested this move, for it wanted a port of its own in Morocco. Kaiser Wilhelm II traveled to Tangier, the capital of Morocco, to assure the sultan of Morocco of his friendship. Britain stood by French aims in the region and helped prevent armed conflict when it organized the Algeciras Conference of 1906. The Algeciras Conference divided control of Morocco between the French and the Spanish, and refused to allow the Germans to establish a port there. It was a stinging rebuke for Germany, which had wanted to extend its power into North Africa.

A bigger crisis between the European powers developed in 1908. The Ottoman Empire, based in Turkey, had long dominated affairs on the Balkan Peninsula, a landmass that included the states and provinces of Serbia, Bosnia, Herzegovina, Montenegro, Bulgaria, Albania, and Greece. The Ottoman Empire's control of the region had been slipping for some time, however. Serbia wanted to extend its influence in the region, and several of the states wanted to become independent. Austria-Hungary, however, did not like the idea of independent Serb countries on its borders; it wanted to keep the Balkan States under its control. In 1908 it annexed (claimed as part of Austria-Hungary) the provinces of Bosnia and Herzegovina. Serbia, which claimed Bosnia and Herzegovina as its own, appealed to Russia for help, and Russia protested Austria-Hungary's actions. At this point the German kaiser announced that he supported his ally and would gladly go to war alongside Austria-Hungary if need be. Russia was not willing to go to war with Germany and backed down. The confrontation left bad blood in the east: Russia was humiliated and determined not to back down again; Serbs in Serbia and within Bosnia and Herzegovina vowed to have their revenge against Austria-Hungary. The stage was set for future troubles in the Balkans.

In 1911 the Morocco issue came back to haunt Europe again. The French broke the agreement made at the Algeciras Conference by trying to establish more direct control over the semi-independent kingdom and Germany, France, and Britain

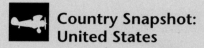

Country Snapshot: United States

- Total population (1913): 97.3 million

- Industrial Potential (1913; Britain in 1900 = 100): 298.1*

- Share of World Manufacturing Output (1913; as percentage of whole): 32.0 percent

- Military and Naval Personnel (1914): 164,000

- Warship Tonnage (1914): 985,000**

(Paul Kennedy, The Rise and Fall of the Great Powers *[New York: Random House, 1987], p. 199.)*

* *This is a relative measure of the strengths of the various economies.*

** *This is a measure of the number of tons of water displaced by a nation's warships.*

all sent or prepared to send troops to the region. The Germans once again looked to gain a foothold in North Africa, and the French and British were determined to keep the Germans out. Three European powers stood on the brink of war. When British prime minister David Lloyd George spoke out against Germany and assured the French that they had full British support, the Germans backed down. But like Russia, they resolved that next time they would not give in to diplomatic pressure.

At the Breaking Point

By the early 1910s the peace that had existed in Europe for the previous forty years was growing increasingly uneasy. Since 1870 the major powers had slowly organized themselves into two competing blocks: the Dual Alliance of Germany and Austria-Hungary, and the Triple Entente of France, Russia, and Great Britain. Each side viewed the actions of the other with suspicion. Germany, which already felt itself surrounded by Russia on its east and France on its west, suspected that the French and British were working together to halt German colonial efforts in Africa. Russia and Austria-Hungary both thought that the Baltic region should be under their control. And now, after the diplomatic clashes over Morocco and the Balkans, the leaders of each country felt compelled to defend the honor of their country.

Each of the major powers had made itself highly capable of waging war; each country had masses of men and military weaponry at the ready. Despite rising antiwar beliefs among the people, there was also a spirit of nationalism in each country. This meant that if leaders decided to go to war, they could count on the support of the people. Military leaders had laid careful plans for how they would wage war; their mobilization schedules stood ready.

Between 1911 and 1914, the prospect of war was in the air. Europe awaited the incident that would provoke leaders to use military force. Not surprisingly, that incident came in the Balkans. Through 1912 and 1913 small wars flared between the Balkan states and provinces. Serbia grew in strength, but neither Austria-Hungary nor Russia intervened. Then, in 1914, a pro-Serbian terrorist from Bosnia assassinated Austrian archduke Franz Ferdinand in Sarajevo. Unwilling to ignore this open assault, Austria-Hungary decided that it must punish Serbia. The alliances locked into place: Germany sided with Austria-Hungary, Russia came to the defense of Serbia, and the French sided with Russia. Within days, Europe was on the brink of war. The next chapter discusses how the assassination of the archduke finally drew all of Europe into war.

For More Information

Bosco, Peter. *World War I.* New York: Facts on File, 1991.

Clare, John D., ed. *First World War.* San Diego, CA: Harcourt Brace, 1995.

Sommerville, Donald. *World War I: History of Warfare.* Austin, TX: Raintree Steck-Vaughn, 1999.

Stewart, Gail. *World War One.* San Diego, CA: Lucent, 1991.

Sources

Ferguson, Niall. *The Pity of War.* New York: Basic Books, 1999.

Haythornthwaite, Philip J. *The World War One Source Book.* London: Arms and Armour Press, 1992.

Kennedy, P. M. *The Rise and Fall of the Great Powers: Economic Change and Military Conflict from 1500 to 2000.* New York: Random House, 1987.

Ross, Stewart. *Causes and Consequences of World War I. Austin, TX: Raintree Steck-Vaughn, 1998.*

Stokesbury, James L. *A Short History of World War I.* New York: William Morrow, 1981.

2 Setting the World on Fire: The Start of World War I

On June 28, 1914, Archduke Franz Ferdinand (1863–1914) of Austria, the heir to the Austrian throne, and his wife, Countess Sophie, paid an official visit to Sarajevo, the provincial capital of Bosnia-Herzegovina. Bosnia and Herzegovina had been annexed (claimed) by the Austro-Hungarian Empire in 1908, but Serbians within Bosnia-Herzegovina, encouraged by the neighboring country of Serbia, rebelled against Austro-Hungarian rule in frequent protests and civil disturbances. The Serbs did not like Austria-Hungary's claim to Bosnia-Herzegovina, which they thought should belong to them. Archduke Franz Ferdinand's visit, which included a review of Austrian troop strength in the province, was intended to remind protestors of the power of Austria-Hungary. Instead, it offered Serbian rebels the chance they needed to start a war.

Franz Ferdinand and his wife set off on their tour of Sarajevo in a convertible car with the top down. Despite warnings of an assassination plot, the couple had little protection. Soon the warnings became reality. A member of the Black Hand, a Serbian terrorist group, launched a small bomb toward

the car. The driver of the car sped forward; Sophie ducked; and Franz Ferdinand knocked the bomb off the back of the car and into the street behind him. The bomb exploded, destroying the next car and wounding several of its occupants and some bystanders. Franz Ferdinand continued on, passing by several other would-be assassins, each of whom missed his opportunity to kill the archduke.

After a brief speech by the shaken mayor at the town hall, the royal party continued on its auto tour. Their first stop was to be the hospital where the injured people from the morning's bombing were taken, but the chauffeur did not know the way. After taking a wrong turn, he stopped to turn the car around. Standing nearby was Gavrilo Princip (1894–1918), a nineteen-year-old Bosnian student and the lone remaining hope of the Black Hand plot. Princip stepped onto the running board of the archduke's car, raised his pistol, and fired two shots. Historian James L. Stokesbury describes the scene in *A Short History of World War I:* "The Archduke

German soldiers kissing their families goodbye during army mobilization.
Reproduced by permission of Archive Photos, Inc.

The borders of Germany, Austria-Hungary, and Turkey in 1914. *Reproduced by permission of The Gale Group.*

opened his mouth and a gout of blood spilled over his tunic. He turned to his wife, begged her not to die, and collapsed. He had been shot in the neck. She was hit in the lower stomach and bleeding internally; she was already dead. Within minutes, so was he." Police seized Princip immediately and hauled him off to prison; in the commotion Princip was unable to swallow the cyanide pill he had carried which would have guaranteed him a quick death.

Austria-Hungary's Decision

The assassination of Franz Ferdinand and his wife was an affront that demanded an answer. But how would Austria act? Would this single event be enough to bring the long-simmering tensions in Europe to a boil? (See Chapter 1 for a description of those tensions.) In the month after the assassination, the response of Austria-Hungary and all the other powers in Europe would turn this single event in a distant province into the spark that started World War I.

Franz Ferdinand and his wife were quickly buried. Some within the Austrian Empire were not sad to see him go. This nephew of Austrian emperor Franz Josef I had few friends in positions of power and had been widely distrusted by those close to the emperor. Some within the emperor's administration hoped that a quick investigation and prosecution of the terrorists would settle the issue. But others saw the assassination as an opportunity for Austria-Hungary to teach Serbia a lesson and gain more power in the Balkans (a group of coun-

Police apprehending Gavrilo Princip after he assassinated Crown Prince Franz Ferdinand and his wife Sophie with a fatal shot at close range. *Reproduced by permission of Corbis Corporation (Bellevue).*

Gavrilo Princip: Killer or Hero?

Little is known of Gavrilo Princip (1894–1918), whose murder of Austrian archduke Franz Ferdinand on June 28, 1914, is said to have started World War I. One of nine children born to a postman in Obljaj, Bosnia, Princip was never a healthy youth. He attended high school in Sarajevo and Tuzla but traveled to Belgrade in 1912 to attend schools that promoted Serbian nationalism. It was his commitment to Serb nationalism that led Princip to become an assassin.

At the time of the assassination, Serbia had recently freed itself from nearly five hundred years of rule by the Turkish Ottoman Empire and was eager to gather all the Serbs in the region into a single country. Serbia bitterly resented the power of the Austro-Hungarian Empire and urged Serbs within Bosnia and Herzegovina, an Austrian province, to resist Austro-Hungarian rule. Serbs hoped that one day Bosnia and Herzegovina would become part of a greater Serbia. Princip hoped that he could encourage revolution against Austria-Hungary by assassinating the Archduke.

Princip was one of six youthful Bosnian members of the Black Hand, a pro-Serbian terrorist group, who lined the streets on June 28, 1914, to attempt to assassinate the archduke. The first would-be assassin, Nedeljko Cabrinovic, lofted a grenade that bounced off the archduke's car and wounded nearly twenty people. Speeding away from this first attack, the archduke passed by Princip and the other attackers without incident. But Princip soon found himself in the right place at the right time when the archduke's car came to a stop right in front of him. Without pause Princip stepped forward and fired the shots that started the war.

Princip was quickly grabbed by police, who probably saved him from murder at the hands of the crowd. He, Cabrinovic, and twenty-three others were eventually tried for plotting the assassination. The Austrian prosecutors who oversaw the trial tried to pin blame on the Serbs, but Princip refused to reveal any assistance he may have received.

tries occupying the Balkan Peninsula, including Bosnia-Herze-govina and Serbia as well as Bulgaria, Rumania, Greece, and Turkey). The leader of Austria's armed forces, General Franz Conrad von Hötzendorf, was ready to wage war on Serbia—a war he had longed for. And Conrad von Hötzendorf (often known simply as Conrad) had the ear of the emperor.

Conrad and others within the Austrian military

Gavrilo Princip. *Reproduced by permission of Archive Photos, Inc.*

Princip's final statement in court, as documented in the court proceedings, was brief: "In trying to insinuate that someone else has instigated the assassination, one strays from the truth. The idea arose in our own minds, and we ourselves executed it. We have loved the people. I have nothing to say in my defense." Princip was sentenced to life in

prison. He died of tuberculosis just a few years later, on April 28, 1918, in the Theresienstadt prison.

Since his death, Princip has been lauded as a hero or hated as a villain, depending on the political situation in his homeland. After World War II, Communist leader Josip Tito hailed Princip as a socialist hero and established a museum in his honor in Sarajevo in 1953. The spot where Princip was standing when he fired the fatal bullets was memorialized with footprints set in concrete. But when Serb soldiers began their attack on Sarajevo during regional conflict in the Balkans in 1992, non-Serbian residents of the city destroyed the Princip museum and the memorial footprints as ugly reminders of Serb dominance. In 2000, journalist David DeVoss could find few traces of the museum or the reputation of one of Europe's most famous assassins. Whether Princip will appear again as a Serbian hero depends in large part on the shifting political currents in a region that has endured nearly a century of conflict.

blamed Serbia for the assassination. The terrorist group behind the attack, the Black Hand, was led by Colonel Dragutin Dimitrijevic, the head of Serbian military intelligence; and the Serbian ambassador to Austria seemed to have known about the assassination plot beforehand. To the Austrians, this was evidence enough that Serbia was trying to undermine Austrian power in Bosnia-Herzegovina. Before Austria-Hungary entered into war, however, it wanted to check with Germany. (Germany and Austria-Hungary had been allied for years; for details on their alliance, see Chapter 1.)

On July 5, Emperor Franz Josef wrote to Kaiser Wilhelm, the leader of Germany, seeking his support for Austro-Hungarian efforts against Serbia: "The bloody deed was not the work of a single individual but a well organized plot whose threads extend to Belgrade [the capital of Serbia].... [T]here can be no doubt that its policy of uniting all Southern Slavs under the Serbian flag encourages such crimes and the continuation of this situation is a chronic peril for my House and my territories. My efforts must be directed to isolating Serbia and reducing her size," wrote Franz Josef, as quoted by Jay Winter and Blaine Baggett in *The Great War and the Shaping of the 20th Century*. The Germans assured the Austro-Hungarians that they had Germany's full backing; neither side thought that Russia would be willing to go to war to protect its Serbian ally. The stage was set for Austria to act.

The Austrian Ultimatum

Had Austria-Hungary attacked Serbia right away, World War I might never have happened. After all, Austria-Hungary would only have been avenging an act of terrorism for which most nations, including Russia, believed Serbia was responsible. But Austria-Hungary did not act right away. Hungarians within the government did not want an all-out war, and they restrained the Austrians. What Austria-Hungary did instead was issue an ultimatum, a diplomatic message that promised penalties if certain conditions were not met. The Austrian ultimatum of July 23, 1914, presented a long list of demands. The Serbian government was asked to renounce all anti-Austrian propaganda (information provided to convince people of a viewpoint), to arrest and punish any Serbian officials involved in the assassination, and to allow Austro-Hungarian officials to enter Serbia to oversee the investigation within Serbia. The Serbian government agreed to most of the conditions, but they could not allow Austria-Hungary to conduct an investigation on Serbian soil; it would amount to giving up Serbia's self-governance. Therefore, on July 25, the Serbians offered their partial acceptance of the ultimatum and proposed that the problem items be open to discussion. The Austro-Hungarians, who insisted that the Serbs accept the entire ultimatum, took the Serb response as a complete rejection of the ultimatum and decided to go to war.

The Coming of War

Following Serbia's refusal of the Austro-Hungarian ultimatum, events moved very quickly. Russia decided that it must not allow its Serbian ally to be attacked, and on July 25 Russia issued a preliminary mobilization order—in other words, it asked its armed forces to prepare to go to war. On July 25 the French government promised to support its Russian allies. (For more on European alliances, see Chapter 1.) On July 26 Great Britain offered to help settle the dispute before it turned into war, but Austria declared that the dispute was now a matter of national honor and refused to enter into a diplomatic discussion. Though Germany had hoped to avoid war, it was ready to honor its commitment to Austria and awaited the beginning of hostilities to prompt its troops into action.

On July 28, 1914, Austria declared war on Serbia. Though few Austrian troops were prepared to go into battle, the Austrians began an artillery bombardment of the Serbian capital of Belgrade the next day. According to Winter and Baggett, the Russian foreign minister announced to the Austrian ambassador, "This means a European war. You are setting Europe alight." He was soon proved correct. Nicholas II, czar (also spelled *tsar;* leader) of Russia, ordered the Russian military to mobilize for war—then quickly withdrew his order when the Germans indicated that they would try to hold off the Austrians. But Russian mobilization was on again by July 30, fueled by the Russian generals' desire to go to war. The next day Germany offered Russia an ultimatum of its own: halt Russian mobilization or the Germans would declare war on Russia. When the Russians ignored the ultimatum, Germany declared war on Russia on August 1. Austria declared war on Russia on August 6.

France and Britain Jump In

The involvement of Germany and Russia in the conflict between Austria-Hungary and Serbia was nearly inevitable. Germany had openly declared its support for the Austro-Hungarian Empire, and Russia had deep cultural ties to Serbia that it felt compelled to honor. If Russia went to war with Germany, French involvement was also inevitable, for France had been an ally of Russia since 1894, when the two countries joined in an alliance in which they shared military plans and forged strong economic links. Their goal was to contain the growing power of the German and Austro-Hungarian alliance. Even had Germany not openly attacked France in the early days of the war, the French would have joined with the Russians.

Britain had no such formal alliance with France or Russia, but it preferred those countries to the Germans and had agreed to assist France in the case of German aggression. Germany hoped to avoid British involvement, for it did not want to have to fight Great Britain as well. Early on, Germany offered not to keep any French or Belgian territory it gained in war if the British would remain neutral, but Britain refused this offer. On August 3 German troops crossed over into tiny Luxembourg and neutral Belgium to begin their attack on France, and Britain declared war on Germany the next day.

Within days of the Austrian bombing of Belgrade, all of the major combatants had declared war. Throughout Europe, people believed that this war would be like the others that had periodically erupted in Europe over the last half century: short and not terribly bloody. The war plans of every country called for a short campaign, and most expected that, following a brief period of fighting, the diplomats would settle issues and peace would return. But the conditions that had allowed for short wars no longer existed, and Europe—and the rest of the world—soon found itself in a much larger war than the various countries had imagined when making their ill-fated war plans.

War Plans

Leading the charge to war in each of the combatant countries were military leaders who were eager to test war plans they had spent years preparing. War plans were detailed instructions for how a country's generals should conduct a war; the plans dictated how many troops should be sent to which areas and in which order. By far the most complicated and ambitious of the war plans belonged to Germany. The German war plan was known as the Schlieffen plan, named after Count Alfred von Schlieffen (1833–1913), who was chief of the

The Schlieffen Plan, 1914.
Reproduced by permission of The Gale Group.

German general staff from 1891 to 1905. Schlieffen predicted that Germany would one day be involved in a two-front war against France and Russia (a front is an area of contact between opposing forces in battle). The Schlieffen plan offered a way for Germany to win such a war by first defeating the French and then turning their attention to the Russians.

In the preparatory phase of the Schlieffen plan, Germany would draw the French forces forward in the Alsace-Lorraine region of Germany (which had once belonged to France). As French forces committed themselves to battle in the east, the main German force would cross Luxembourg and Belgium and begin entering France all along its northeastern border. Sweeping southward and westward, the Germans would quickly capture Paris (the French capital), cut off French supply lines, and encircle the entire French army. Once they had defeated the French army, the Germans would speed back across Germany on its well-developed rail system and defeat the Russians, who might not yet be organized enough to do battle.

The Schlieffen plan depended on a series of conditions falling into place. First, it assumed that the French would be ready for war quickly and the Russians more slowly; thus, the Germans assumed that they could fight their enemies one at a time. Second, the plan relied on German speed in extending its force all the way to the coast of the English Channel for the push to encircle the French army. The plan failed to account for British involvement, which would naturally come at the far western reaches of the front. If all worked well, however, "the Germans thought the Schlieffen plan guaranteed them victory within three or four months," according to James L. Stokesbury in *A Short History of World War I.* However, as Stokesbury notes, "what it really guaranteed was that if for some reason they did not win within that time, they would ultimately lose the war."

Austro-Hungarian war plans were not nearly as advanced as those of Germany, but Austria-Hungary also expected that it might have to face the enemy on two fronts. In the southeast, Austria-Hungary would certainly face the Serbs, but the assumed weakness of the Serbian forces allowed Austria-Hungary to post a significant portion of its forces on the northeast frontier with Russia and along the border with Poland. Austro-Hungarian war planners believed that they could quickly shift their troops to the front where they were needed most; in practice, however, this meant that huge numbers of their troops spent the early part of the war marching back and forth between the two fronts, awaiting action. According to Stokesbury, "the Austrians did their best to wear out their armies as soon as possible."

Unlike the Germans, the French could not agree on the best plans for war. In the years before the war, prominent generals had argued over how to prepare for a war with Germany. One-time commander in chief General Victor Michel guessed that the German attack would come through Belgium and proposed that the first French action should be to cut off the Germans in Belgium before they could reach French territory. Michel's plan, which was unpopular with political leaders but turned out to be absolutely correct, cost him his job. His replacement, General Joseph Joffre (1852–1931), called instead for a direct attack on German positions in the formerly French territories of Alsace-Lorraine. (He called for a smaller force to monitor German activities in Belgium.) Joffre's plan was adopted by his country, and it left France highly vulnerable to the German Schlieffen plan. Joffre also underestimated the number of German troops the French armies would face and overestimated the impact that Russian battles would have on the conflict. Joffre's faulty vision of how the war would unfold cost the French dearly in the early stages of the conflict.

The British had not been involved in a war on the European continent in decades, and they were uncertain about how they wanted to commit forces there. Their lone plan was to send an expeditionary force of roughly 100,000 men to assist French troops in any battles they might face on their left flank, the area nearest the coast. Britain asked France to name the minimum number of British troops it would like. According to Stokesbury, French politician Georges Clemenceau (1841–1929), unimpressed by the British commitment to the war effort, famously replied, "One, and we shall take good care to get him killed." The thousands of British troops sent to the Continent did in fact die in large numbers during the war.

Mobilization

With war declared, all of Europe prepared for what many thought of as a grand adventure. The soldiers in most of the countries had never seen battle, for Europe had largely been at peace since 1871. But they had heard countless stories about the glory of war and about the honor that would come to soldiers who defended their country. Thus, in the first days of August 1914, much of Europe found itself caught up in the rush of mobilization—the preparation of men and machines for battle.

Across France, Germany, Austria-Hungary, and Russia, reservists—trained soldiers who were not serving on active duty—were called to report for service. Throughout the country posters appeared calling reservists to their duty. By the hundreds of thousands, these men left their jobs, farms, and families and reported to military stations; there they exchanged the soft clothes of civilian life for coarse and often ill-fitting military uniforms. Altogether, some four million Russians, three million Austro-Hungarians, four-and-a-half million Germans, and four million French reported for duty.

The sheer scale of mobilization served as a warning about the war-waging capacity of modern nations. During mobilization, the Germans scheduled the movement of troops and supplies on some 11,000 trains; the French, on their less developed railway system, marshaled 7,000 trains into service. Across the warring countries, trains moved at a brisk, efficient pace, carrying men onward to the front. Equally impressive was the number of horses gathered for military service. According to John Keegan, author of *The First World War,* "Even Britain's little army called up 165,000 [horses], mounts for the cavalry and draught animals for the artillery and regimental transport wagons. The Austrian army mobilized 600,000, the German 715,000, the Russian—with its twenty-four cavalry divisions—over a million."

Off to War!

In cities throughout Europe, the rush to war was greeted with enthusiasm and patriotism. French ambassador to Russia Maurice Paléologue marveled at the devotion that the inhabitants of the Russian city of St. Petersburg showed in responding to the Czar's call to war. Keegan quotes Paléologue: "An enormous crowd had congregated with flags, banners, icons and portraits of the Tsar. The Emperor appeared on the balcony. The entire crowd at once knelt and sang the Russian national anthem. To those thousands of men on their knees at that moment the Tsar was really the autocrat appointed of God, the military, political and religious leader of his people, the absolute master of their bodies and souls." Austrian soldier Adolf Hitler (1889–1945)—who would later gain notoriety as the leader of Germany's Nazi Party—claimed that "[I was] not ashamed to acknowledge that I was carried away by the enthusiasm of the moment and ... sank down upon my knees and thanked Heaven out of the fullness of my heart for the favour of having been permitted to live in such times," according to Keegan. Most Europeans believed in the wisdom of their rulers and gladly obeyed their call to war.

In France, the departure of troop trains to the front occurred in an atmosphere of celebration. A French soldier quoted in Keegan's *The First World War* remembered the scene:

At six in the morning, without any signal, the train slowly steamed out of the station. At that moment, quite spontaneously, like a smouldering fire suddenly erupting into roaring flames, an immense clamour arose as the Marseillaise *[a French anthem] burst from a thousand throats. All the men were standing at the train's windows, waving their kepis [caps]. From the track, quais [quays] and the neighbouring trains, the crowds waved back.... Crowds gathered at every station, behind every barrier, and at every window along the road. Cries of "Vive la France! Vive l'armée" ["Long live France! Long live the army"] could be heard everywhere, while people waved handkerchiefs and hats. The women were throwing kisses and heaped flowers on our convoy. The young men were shouting: "Au revoir! Bientôt!" ["Goodbye! See you soon!"]*

Kaiser Wilhelm, the German leader, told his departing troops that they would be home "before the leaves have fallen from the trees," according to Zachary Kent, author of *World War I: "The War to End Wars."* Little did people know that millions of soldiers would never return to their homes, for the war that the soldiers happily marched off to was not the limited war of the nineteenth century but a new kind of war altogether: modern, mechanized warfare, which slaughtered millions and seemed to drag on forever.

The Clash Begins

After drawing the French forces forward in the Alsace-Lorraine region of Germany, along France's eastern border, Germany's plan was to cross Belgium in order to attack the French on their northeast border. Germany asked Belgium for free passage across its countryside; the Belgians refused and thus became Germany's first target. The Germans declared war on Belgium on August 4 and almost simultaneously attacked the Belgian fortress town of Liège. The Belgian army, commanded by King Albert I (1875–1934), was willing to fight, but they had never planned to counter an army as strong as Germany's. From a string of solidly built forts surrounding the city, the Belgians fought off the German army. On August 12, however, the Germans finally brought their large artillery (mounted guns that shoot large shells) into the battle, and these large guns proceeded to smash the forts to rubble. By August 16 Belgian resistance at Liège was destroyed, and the Germans began their march across the Belgian countryside.

After destroying Liège, the Germans moved more quickly across Belgium, facing scattered resistance from the

Belgian army. By the end of the third week in August, German forces were approaching the border that divides Belgium and France. France had also launched its first attacks in accordance with its war plan, clashing with the German army in the Alsace-Lorraine region on August 14. By the third week in August, the warring countries found themselves preparing to fight across a broad front that stretched from Switzerland all the way to the Belgian coast on the North Sea. The Germans were preparing to push into France, while the French were joined by the British Expeditionary Force in preparing to counter the German attack. Far to the east, Russian troops prepared to sweep into Germany. War had begun. In the weeks and months to come, all sides would see their war plans in tatters and their goals of speedy victory dashed. They would soon be locked into a war unlike any the world had seen before.

For More Information

Bosco, Peter. *World War I.* New York: Facts on File, 1991.

Clare, John D., ed. *First World War.* San Diego, CA: Harcourt Brace, 1995.

Ross, Stewart. *Causes and Consequences of World War I.* Austin, TX: Raintree Steck-Vaughn, 1998.

Sommerville, Donald. *World War I: History of Warfare.* Austin, TX: Raintree Steck-Vaughn, 1999.

Stewart, Gail. *World War One.* San Diego, CA: Lucent, 1991.

Sources

DeVoss, David. "Searching for Gavrilo Princip." *Smithsonian* (August 2000).

Keegan, John. *The First World War.* New York: Alfred A. Knopf, 1999.

Kent, Zachary. *World War I: "The War to End Wars."* Hillside, NJ: Enslow, 1994.

Stokesbury, James L. *A Short History of World War I.* New York: William Morrow, 1981.

Winter, Jay, and Blaine Baggett. *The Great War and the Shaping of the 20th Century.* New York: Penguin Studio, 1996.

The World War I Document Archive. [Online] http://www.ukans.edu/~kansite/ww_one/ (accessed October 2000).

Settling In: The First Years on the Western Front

3

Worl War I began on August 4, 1914, with Germany and France launching their attacks according to the war plans they had carefully laid out during peacetime. Germany crossed Belgium and began its attack on France along that country's northeastern border; France sent its forces against German foes in the Alsace region; Great Britain sent help across the English Channel to bolster French forces. Within weeks, however, it became obvious that this war would not go as planned. The warring armies faced each other along a front that was known at the western front, a line that stretched northwest from Switzerland and eventually reached the Belgian coast. Along the western front German troops were stalled by stiff resistance from the Allies; and French attacks were being repulsed by German machine guns. And there they sat, brutally fighting over small stretches of land, gaining a mile here, 300 yards there, in a bloody confrontation that would last for four more years.

This chapter covers the fighting along the Western Front during the first two years of the war, from the opening of the war in August 1914 to the end of the Battle of the Somme in the autumn of 1916. Despite the important battles that were fought

Howitzer "Big Bertha" being fired. *Reproduced by permission of Archive Photos, Inc.*

in eastern Germany, Russia, Serbia, and in other spots around the globe, the fighting on the Western Front is considered the most important in the war. It was on the Western Front that the major combatants committed the majority of their troops and their efforts. And it was on the Western Front that the world was introduced to a new form of warfare that exhausted nations and destroyed armies on a scale never seen before.

Prelude to War: The March across Belgium

At the war's outset, German advances went according to plan—the Schlieffen plan. Created by former chief of the German military Alfred von Schlieffen (1833–1913), the Schlieffen plan called for German troops to storm across Belgium and begin attacking France along its border with Belgium. Germany planned to push the French southwest from the Belgian border and then flank (attack the side of) French troops on the

west, capture the French capital of Paris, and then encircle and defeat the French army.(Then, Germany would be free to battle Russia in the east; see Chapter 5.) Schlieffen's plan required two things: massive numbers of German troops and speed. Yet Helmuth Johannes von Moltke (1848–1916), the chief of the German general staff (the ruling body of the military) from 1906 to 1914, decided not to commit as many troops as Schlieffen had called for at the far western edge of the German attack. It was a crucial mistake.

Germany asked for free passage across Belgium; the Belgians refused, and Germany decided to fight its way across. Belgium was a neutral country; it did not have a large army. But it did have a complex of fortresses near the town of Liège, squarely in the path of the German advance. On August 4 Germany declared war on Belgium and sent a special attack force to capture Liège. After nearly two weeks of battle and artillery bombardment, Liège was beaten into submission, and the Germans were free to roll across Belgium, facing only scattered resistance

Dead American soldier tangled in barbed wire fence in northern Europe. *Reproduced by permission of Archive Photos, Inc.*

American soldiers climbing up out of the trenches.
Reproduced by permission of Archive Photos, Inc.

from snipers and small bands of troops. On August 19 the Germans began their attack on Belgium's fortress at Namur, and the next day they entered Brussels, the nation's capital.

The German advance turned the peaceful countryside into a fierce battlefield. A French officer observed this change from a point near the Belgium-France border, as quoted in Martin Gilbert's *The First World War: A Complete History:* "A dog was barking at some sheep. A girl was singing as she walked down the lane behind us. From a little farm away on the right came the voices and laughter of some soldiers cooking their evening meal . . . Then, without a moment's warning, with a suddenness that made us start and strain our eyes to see what our minds could not realize, we saw the whole horizon burst into flame." A German artillery attack had begun. "A chill of horror came over us," the soldier continued. "War seemed suddenly to have assumed a merciless, ruthless aspect that we had not realized till then. Hitherto it had been war as we had conceived it, hard blows, straight dealing, but now for the first

time we felt as if some horrible Thing, utterly merciless, was advancing to grip us." That terrible Thing, modern warfare, would soon grip the entire Western Front.

First French Attacks

The French also opened the war according to plan—in their case, Plan XVII. Unlike the detailed Schlieffen plan, writes James L. Stokesbury in *A Short History of World War I*, the French plan "was more a statement of general intent. It called for the concentration forward of all the French armies, and then for them to move to the attack as they were fully mobilized." Under General Joseph "Papa" Joffre (1852–1931), the French launched their first attack on the town of Mulhouse in the Alsace region of Germany. It was a botched attack led by a reluctant commander who was soon fired by Joffre.

A more sustained French offensive was launched on August 14, 1914. For six days, French troops pushed into the

The first major attacks of
German and Allied forces at
the outbreak of World War I
in 1914. *Reproduced by
permission of The Gale Group.*

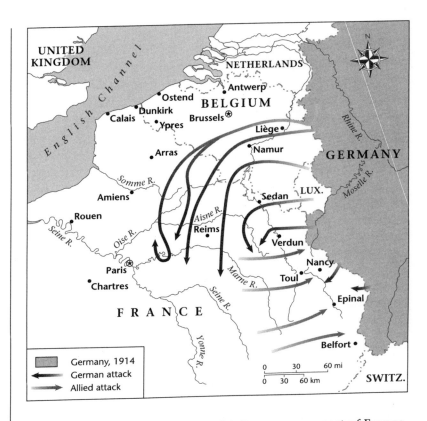

German province of Lorraine, which was once a part of France. Dressed in their bright red trousers and blue coats and waving their bayonets before them, the French soldiers poured forward in neat lines. Despite being hammered by German machine-gunfire, they still managed to advance. On August 20, however, the German forces launched a brutal counterattack. The two sides fought through the day, and the exhausted French began a retreat that night. The Germans pressed the French through the night, and for the next two days pushed them all the way back across the French border and nearly to the city of Nancy. The first French offensives had failed, and the southeastern end of the front locked into place. The next battles would take place to the north and west.

The Battles of the Frontier

The opening French attacks in the Alsace-Lorraine region failed. Even worse, French generals realized to their

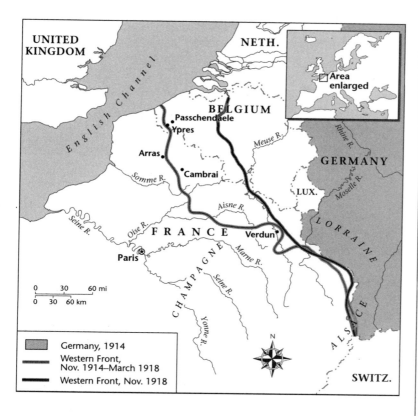

The Western Front from November 1914–March 1918, as well as Western Front in November 1918. *Reproduced by permission of The Gale Group.*

horror that German armies approaching through Belgium were near the French border. Joffre sent the French Third, Fourth, and Fifth armies into the Ardennes region, which lay east of the Meuse River. On August 22, in this hilly, wooded valley the French Third and Fourth armies met German troops of surprising strength. The French were badly beaten, with infantry abandoning the field in panic under the assault of German artillery. The most experienced of the French divisions, the Third Colonial, suffered 11,000 casualties (men killed, wounded, or taken prisoner) out of a total of 15,000 soldiers.

The next major confrontation—there were many minor confrontations—occurred near the Belgian town of Mons. French troops under General Charles Lanrezac were to advance into Belgium alongside the newly arrived British Expeditionary Force (BEF) led by Field Marshal Sir John French (1852–1925). But Lanrezac's Fifth Army was driven backward along the Sambre River by the ferocious firepower of German

German army marching into Brussels. *Reproduced by permission of Corbis Corporation (Bellevue).*

troops. By August 23, the French army had decided to retreat, leaving the outmanned British to fight the Battle of Mons.

The Battle of Mons. The 150,000-man British Expeditionary Force (BEF) had arrived in France not long after the British declared war on Germany. By August 23, the British had taken up positions on a front twenty miles wide, facing north toward the town of Mons. (The western front ran generally southeast to northwest. But the front had jigs and jags, allowing some individual battle fronts to be aligned along a north-south axis and others along a more southeast-northwest axis.) Their five divisions would soon face the full force of German general Alexander von Kluck's First Army, fourteen divisions strong (a division was usually made up of a headquarters and three to five brigades of troops). The BEF stood at the far northwestern end of the front; by overrunning them, the Germans could successfully flank the combined French and British forces and achieve the goal of the Schlieffen plan. Instead, the BEF fought one of the bravest battles of the war, slowing the German advance before fleeing again in retreat.

The British soldiers fighting at Mons were experienced professional soldiers, many of whom had fought in the Boer War in Africa some years earlier. They were crack marksmen known for their ability to fire quickly and accurately. Their firepower soon took its toll on the advancing Germans. A German soldier, quoted in John Keegan's *The First World War,* recalled facing the British rifles: "No sooner had we left the edge of the wood than a volley of bullets whistled past our noses and cracked into the trees behind. Five or six cries near me, five or six of my grey lads collapsed in the grass. . . . The firing seemed at long range . . . . Here we were as if advancing on a parade ground. . . . away in front a sharp, hammering sound, then a pause, then a more rapid hammering—machine guns!" But they weren't machine guns—they were British soldiers firing at rapid speed.

With their overwhelming numbers, the Germans eventually pressured the British out of their positions, and the BEF joined the French forces in a general retreat from battle. But they were not through fighting. In fact, British and French forces fought bravely in retreat, especially at Le Cateau, and set the stage for another major confrontation in the Battle of the Marne.

The Battle of the Marne

In the days following the Battle of Mons, the Germans continued pressing forward, driving southwest from Mons directly toward Paris. To some, it looked as though the German plan might succeed, for the Germans were coming perilously close to circling around the Allies. But the problems with the Schlieffen plan soon revealed themselves. The further forward the Germans pushed, the more distance they opened between themselves and their supplies of food and ammunition. Stretched thinly across enemy territory, German troops had difficulty communicating with each other and with their leader, General Moltke. Moltke often did not know which armies were in which positions, and he grew frantic in his efforts to control the actions of the war.

Though they had been pushed back, the French had easy access to supplies and to reinforcements. And their leader, Joffre, grew increasingly confident that French forces would

Joseph "Papa" Joffre.
Reproduced courtesy of the Library of Congress.

French soldiers at the Battle of the Marne. *Reproduced by permission of Archive Photos, Inc.*

withstand the German onslaught. Thus, at the end of the first week in September, the tide of the war shifted. Well fed and well supplied, the French and British armies began an attack of their own in what became known as the Battle of the Marne. Pushing forward, the French encountered disorganized German troops, which soon turned in retreat. In hard-fought battles on September 6 and 7, the French slowly pushed the Germans back to the River Ourcq. According to Stokesbury, "The dead piled up in little villages, and the French put in attack after attack. Many of them were reservists, tired and confused, but they fought on all through the day." Finally, on September 9, the Germans had had enough, and they retreated back beyond the Marne River, north toward Belgium.

The Race to the Sea

The Germans had advanced as far as they could. Sent back northward, they now had to rethink their attack. They still hoped to get around the open flank of the French army to the west; the French saw a similar flank to the German army. And so began the race to the sea, the name given to the series of running battles between two armies desperately trying to outflank the other.

As each side attacked the other, the clashing armies learned that the best way to defend against machine guns and artillery was to dig trenches in the earth. From these trenches defenders could peer out and annihilate attacking soldiers; dug deep enough, the trenches also provided cover from the flesh-ripping shrapnel thrown off by exploding shells. The barbed wire strung in front of the trenches effectively slowed any enemies who avoided the hail of bullets from machine guns or rapid rifle fire. Through September and into October, in fights known as the First Battle of the Aisne and the First Battle of Artois, German, French, British, and Belgian forces—in ever larger numbers—died as they tried to gain some advantage on the enemy. At one point the Belgian army survived a German attack near the Lys River by opening dikes and allowing seawater to flood the low-lying battlefield.

First Ypres. The final battle in the race to the sea took place in late October and is known as the First Battle of Ypres (pronounced EE-per; British soldiers rhymed it with "wipers."). At First Ypres (as the battle came to be known, to distinguish it from Second and Third Ypres), the Germans made one last effort to gain an advantage before winter set in. After launching an artillery bombardment, which was designed to "soften up" the enemy's defenses, the Germans sent their troops across the field to do battle. They were promptly gunned down by British soldiers nestled into the shallow, muddy trenches. Again and again, over twenty-two days, the Germans tried to gain ground; again and again, increasingly fragmented bands of British soldiers repelled their attack. Finally, on November 22, the battle ended.

Stalemate: The End to Hopes of a Quick War

The result of four months of battle on the Western Front can be described in one word: stalemate. The end result of all the grand war plans, dozens of intense battles, and hundreds of thousands of deaths was a line of opposed armies stretching 475 miles from the Belgian coast on the North Sea southeast to the border of neutral Switzerland. In these months of battle, nearly 306,000 French soldiers died; Germany's dead numbered 241,000; Belgium and Great Britain both lost 30,000 men. Worse—if anything could be worse than all these deaths—was the death of any hope that the war would end soon. As the combatants settled down to wait out the winter on the dreary plains of the region known as Flanders, they knew that, come spring, the war would go on.

As the generals and political leaders spent the winter planning how to overcome an enemy holding firm in trenches and armed with powerful machine guns, the soldiers in the trenches did their best to survive. Their perspective on the war was made clear in an event referred to as the Christmas Truce.

The Christmas Truce. Christmas Eve, 1914, brought colder temperatures and occasional snow to the soldiers camped in trenches along the Western Front. But it also brought something rare: a chance to put aside hatred and violence and greet the enemy as a fellowman. Across the length of the front, soldiers heard the enemy launch into a Christmas carol or saw them step out of the trenches to extend a hand of friendship. Jay Winter and Blaine Baggett, authors of *The Great War and the Shaping of the 20th Century*, recount one such incident:

> Along some portions of the German lines, unusual lights began to appear. The British thought the enemy was preparing to attack, but then quickly realized that the Germans were placing Christmas trees adorned with candles on the parapets. Instead of rifle fire came shouts from the Germans. "English soldiers, English soldiers, Happy Christmas! Where are your Christmas trees?"

British rifleman Graham Williams, quoted in *The Great War*, recalled:

> [The Germans] finished their carol and we thought that we ought to retaliate in some way, so we sang "The First Noël," and when we finished that they all began clapping; and then they struck up another favourite of theirs, "O Tannenbaum." And so it went on. First the Germans would sing one of their carols and then we would sing one of ours, until when we started up "O Come All Ye Faithful" the Germans immediately joined in singing the same hymn to the Latin words "Adeste Fidèles." And I thought, well, this was really a most extraordinary thing—two nations both singing the same carol in the middle of the war.

When the leaders heard of this fraternization between the enemies, they immediately ordered that such unwarlike

activity must cease. It did, for the combatants soon returned to the activities of war.

The Plan for 1915

The leaders of the three major warring powers on the Western Front all faced the same question: What do we do now? The British, whose Expeditionary Force (the BEF) had

Douglas Haig. *Reproduced courtesy of the Library of Congress.*

been nearly destroyed, were not eager to concentrate their efforts on the Western Front. While Britain tried to rebuild its army with volunteers, it preferred to use its naval power to strike in faraway places such as Gallipoli, Italy (see Chapter 6). The German generals were divided in their opinions. General Erich von Falkenhayn (1861–1922), who had taken over as chief of the German general staff, wanted to win a war of attrition in the west, wearing down the enemy to the point of exhaustion and killing as many as necessary for a decisive victory. But other leading generals argued that Germany needed to win the war against Russia on the Eastern Front before turning its full attention to the Western Front. In the end, the Germans decided to wage a defensive war, hoping to hold the line in the west. The French had no illusions about what they must do: The war was being fought on their soil; they had to drive the Germans back. Thus France went on the offensive. The dreams of a speedy war had faded; each side now knew that winning this war would be a long and difficult process.

In an offensive war, the attacking power usually looks to strike its enemy at a weak point, or to attack from a position of dominance, such as a hill or a strong fortress. But on the Western Front there were no weak points in the German line and no strong positions from which to launch an attack. The French were thus forced to make headlong charges against the waiting defenses of the Germans. French soldiers began these attacks in the First Battle of Champagne in March of 1915, but they quickly exhausted themselves. Meanwhile, British troops under General Douglas Haig (1861–1928) prepared to aid the French offensive with an attack near the village of Neuve-Chapelle. They opened the battle with a barrage of artillery fire—the standard preparation for troop advance—and sent four British divisions against one German division. The British were proud that they were able to push over half a mile into

German territory, but it had cost them 13,000 casualties. (Casualties are men lost in a battle through death, injury, capture, or desertion.)

The Germans struck back hard in the Second Battle of Ypres, which began on April 22. They intended to capture the bulge, or salient, that the French and British occupied in front of the Belgian town of Ypres, and they planned to use a weapon never before used in war: poison gas (see sidebar). The German attack began with an artillery bombardment. James Stokesbury describes the gas attack that followed (the Algerians and Territorials he mentions are part of the French forces):

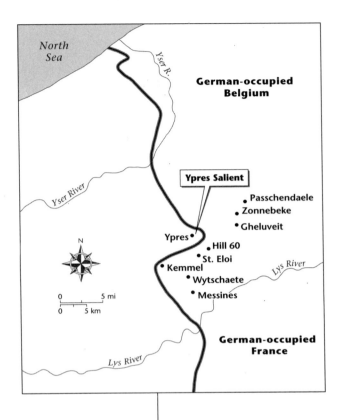

> In the midst of the bombardment a yellowish-green cloud began rolling over the ground toward the French lines. It was chlorine gas, which attacks the lungs and respiratory systems, destroying the mucous membranes of the air passages. As the cloud hit the Algerians' line they broke for the rear; the panic and the gas spread to the Territorials, and they too joined in with their fleeing comrades. Suddenly, there was a hole four miles wide in the Allied line. The Germans pushed boldly forward into this, until they met their own gas—and the Canadians.

The Ypres Salient, 1914-1918. *Reproduced by permission of The Gale Group.*

Though the gas attack had not been decisive, it introduced a new and horrible element into the war. The Germans "won" Second Ypres, pushing French and British forces back several miles. This victory cost Germany 35,000 casualties, and it cost the Allies twice that number. The enemies remained deadlocked.

Joffre's plans for the next French offensive called for his troops to capture a high point called Vimy Ridge near Artois, and he opened the attack in early May. After a five-day artillery bombardment, French troops led by General Henri Philippe Pétain pushed the Germans back two-and-a-half miles. By the time they reached Vimy Ridge, however, the battlefield had become so torn up that it was difficult to bring supplies and reinforcements forward. The Germans repulsed the attack and drove the French down off the ridge. According to

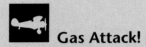

Gas Attack!

Soon after the Germans unleashed poison gas on French troops in the Second Battle of Ypres, such gas attacks, or chemical warfare, became a common feature of World War I battles. Poison gas shells were often launched in the initial artillery barrages that started most battles. The gas that was released spread through the enemy's battle lines, either forcing the soldiers to put on gas masks or forcing them to flee to avoid the disastrous effects of the gas. Gas attacks succeeded because they created chaos among enemy troops.

There were several kinds of gas used in World War I. Tear gas caused temporary blindness and burning of the eyes and throat. Chemical agents that cause asphyxiation (chemical agents which caused choking and suffocation) like chlorine, phosgene, and diphosgene formed hydrochloric acid, which badly burned soldiers' lungs and throats, causing many deaths. The most feared gas was dichlorethylsulfide, or mustard gas. It caused searing burns and blisters on whatever skin it reached. This gas could linger on a battlefield for days.

Gas attacks accounted for 800,000 casualties during the war, most of these on the Western Front. Though the Germans were the first to use gas, they were certainly not the only ones to do so. France, Britain, and the United States all used poison gas in their attacks on the enemy. Poison gas was one of the most hated weapons used in the war. Often invisible, poison gas snuck up on soldiers, suffocating them before they even had a chance to fight back. According to *Great Weapons of World War I* author William G. Dooly Jr., "It symbolized the death of individual bravery, initiative, and skill."

Stokesbury, "the battle degenerated into a simple killing match, and finally both parties subsided after a week." This battle cost France 100,000 men, and the French gained little ground. It was the first of several key battles fought for Vimy Ridge over the course of the war.

Attack . . . Again

By midyear the Allies faced severe shortages of shells and soldiers. Neither the factories nor the military training programs could pump out these "war supplies" quickly enough to satisfy the voracious appetite of battle. Joffre analyzed the situation and decided that the best he could do was try again. And so the French attacked again in the Second Battle of Champagne and the Third Battle of Artois.

The Second Battle of Champagne. The Second Battle of Champagne opened like many other battles: the French first bombed, then charged. This time, however, they broke through the German defenses and pushed behind the German trenches. There they made a sickening discovery: The Germans had dug a second line of trenches. Well supplied and unharmed by French artillery, the German soldiers in this second line of trenches opened fire with their machine guns. French soldiers fell like dominoes. The second line of trenches became the norm on both sides of the battle line, and it further strengthened the defensive capacities of the warring armies. The fight cost the French 145,000 casualties; the Germans, 75,000. But the French gained a little ground, so they declared it a victory. The Third Battle of Artois was similarly inconclusive: The French took Vimy Ridge, the Germans drove them back off it, many men were killed, and the two exhausted armies faced each other across a field of dead.

The Battle of Loos. To the north, the British launched what would become one of the bloodiest battles of the war, the Battle of Loos. Led by General Haig, the British army consisted of both seasoned soldiers and a mass of new recruits freshly trained in Britain. On September 25 the Brits began their bombardment. Next, they released 150 tons of poison chlorine gas, which blew across the no-man's-land between the armies. The British army confidently advanced behind their gas and artillery attack; according to Gilbert, "one battalion was led in its assault by men dribbling a football across No-Man's Land."

The British broke the Germans' first line of defense, occupied their trenches, and prepared for a second push. It was to be their undoing. Climbing out of the trenches by the thousands and advancing across the open field in neat lines, the numerically superior British were riddled with bullets from German machine guns. A German account of the battle, quoted by Gilbert, describes the scene: "The men stood on the fire-steps (of the trenches), some even on the parapets, and fired triumphantly into the mass of men advancing across open grass-land. As the entire field of fire was covered with the enemy's infantry the effect was devastating and they could be seen falling literally in the hundreds." Another German soldier, also quoted by Gilbert, wrote this description in his diary: "[D]ense masses of the enemy, line after line, appeared over the ridges, some of the officers even mounted on horseback and advancing as if carrying out a field-day drill in peacetime. Our ... machine guns riddled their ranks as they came on. As they crossed the northern front of the Bois Hugo, the machine guns caught them in the flank and whole battalions were annihilated."

Like no other, the Battle of Loos confirmed the killing power of the machine gun. The Germans, badly outnumbered and in retreat, had saved the battle by placing machine guns in defensive positions. Both sides were aghast at the numbers of dead; of the 10,000 British involved in the battle, over 8,000 were killed or wounded. The Germans called the battle "Der Leichenfeld von Loos"—the Field of Corpses of Loos.

Loos was bad, but then so was the entire year of battle on the Western Front. By year's end, the British had lost 279,000 men and seen the British Expeditionary Force, once the core of the British army, utterly destroyed; the Germans had lost 612,000. The French, who had led the attacks throughout the year, had 1,292,000 casualties in 1915. Despite all these deaths, little had been decided. The enemies still faced each other across a front that had shifted only slightly from the year before.

1916: The Year of the "Great" Battles

The battles of 1915 brought little change on the Western Front and even less change in the minds of the military leaders, who used the break from war provided by winter to plan for the next year. German general Falkenhayn saw one good thing in the battles of 1915: the extreme loss of French lives. Resentment toward the war was growing in France, and Falkenhayn thought Germany could stop France's desire to fight by raising the cost of waging war. In Falkenhayn's own blunt words, quoted by Stokesbury, the Germans' plan was "to bleed France white." The first step of this plan was to capture the strategic French fortress at Verdun.

French leaders were aware of the costs of waging war, but the idea of giving up did not occur to them. After all, they were fighting to protect their native soil. At a meeting of the Allied leaders late in 1915, the French generals continued to urge new and bigger attacks. The British commander, Douglas Haig, still wished that he had more time to train the recruits who were slowly fleshing out the British army, but as the British had done throughout the war, he followed the French lead. The Allied leaders agreed that they would mount a major offensive near the Somme River.

The Battles of Verdun and of the Somme have gone down in history as two of the "greatest" battles of the war, perhaps of all wars. They are known not as decisive victories, however, but as examples of the tragedy and futility of modern warfare. Verdun is best known for its length—ten months—its cost in lives, and for the introduction of the flamethrower. The Somme is known, especially in Britain, for the sheer efficiency with which men were killed. Both battles finally taught the generals crucial lessons about how to wage a modern war.

 ## No-Man's-Land

In World War I the most haunted and dangerous piece of land was not a battlefield or bombed-out town, but a small strip of land that separated the trenches of the two warring armies—no-man's-land.

No-man's-land could be as narrow as a hundred yards or as wide as a couple of miles. On either side of this strip of land, soldiers had dug trenches and machine-gun nests, strung barbed wire, and stashed the guns and ammunition they would need to kill the enemy. No man dared enter this strip during daylight, for snipers from both sides turned it into a killing zone. During the night, brave soldiers sometimes tried to extend their defenses further into this zone, but they had to be careful to show no light or they too might be killed. No-man's-land was at its worst during and after a battle, for the men who crossed it were killed in vast numbers and their blood soaked the ground. For years after the war, farmers plowing the battlefields of France and Belgium churned up the bones and bullets of men killed in no-man's-land.

The Battle of Verdun

Falkenhayn targeted Verdun because he knew that it was key to French morale: For centuries, some of the greatest battles in French military history had been fought there. In 1916, however, Verdun consisted of a set of forts in a forgotten area of the Western Front. If the Germans could concentrate their forces there and pound their way through, they might be able to finally break the French will to fight. The German attack began

French dugouts near Verdun. *Reproduced by permission of Archive Photos, Inc.*

on February 12 with the biggest artillery barrage bombardment of the war. According to Winter and Baggett, "One million shells were fired on the first day alone." By the end of the battle, over forty million shells would be expended.

As the shelling finished, German troops advanced, causing heavy French losses. The Germans used heavy amounts of phosgene gas and introduced a new weapon to the war: the flamethrower. The flamethrower could shoot flames into trenches or passageways in fortifications, burning alive all those inside. (It could also backfire, as a battalion of German soldiers found when barrels of fuel for the flamethrowers ignited within a section of the fort they occupied, killing over a thousand men.) Within a few days the Germans had taken Fort Vaux and Fort Douaumont, and they boasted that the battle would soon be over.

The French had different ideas. Although they had retreated, they soon were fighting from defensive positions of strength and were able to concentrate their artillery fire on the very spots their troops had recently occupied. Joffre, realizing that he needed a defensive genius to lead the French forces, called on Philippe Pétain (1856–1951). Pétain quickly realized that the way to beat back the German attack was to keep his troops fresh and well supplied. Supplies came forward from the French interior on a road known as the "Voie Sacrée," or Sacred Way. Day and night, this road was clogged with trucks bringing soldiers, shells, and food to the front, and carrying the wounded and the tired back to safety. Constantly shifting men in and out of action may have saved the French army from giving up. It certainly made sure that everyone got to see action in this most important of French battles; historians estimate that 70 percent of the entire French army fought at Verdun at some point in the battle. In the end, Pétain rallied the French soldiers, convincing them that they could not be defeated. For his efforts, he became known as the "Hero of Verdun."

The Battle of Verdun raged on. In the first months of the battle, the Germans were on the offensive, launching attacks here and there across the wide battlefield, taking ground only to lose it to French troops days later. By July the Germans were ready to withdraw from the field, content with having at least achieved the deaths of many Frenchmen. But the French were not willing to let the battle end. Having stocked up on supplies, they began an offensive of their own on October 19, eventually retaking Forts Vaux and Douaumont. By the time the battle ended in the third week in December, the French had retaken nearly all of the territory they had lost.

Was France bled white by the Battle of Verdun, as the Germans hoped? France had lost about 542,000 casualties, but the French army had somehow held itself together, despite the enormous pressures of this months-long battle. Pétain emerged a hero, and he would become the most effective of French generals in battles to come. Germany was nearly bled white itself, having lost 434,000 casualties of its own. The architect of the Battle of Verdun, General von Falkenhayn, was dismissed from his position and replaced by General Paul von Hindenburg, with Erich Ludendorff as his assistant. Hindenburg and Ludendorff were to see the war through to its end.

French soldier falling after being shot in no-man's-land near Verdun. *Reproduced by permission of Corbis Corporation (Bellevue).*

The Battle of the Somme

To the north and west of Verdun, the French and British planned their joint offensive in the area near the Somme River, on a 30-mile front between Amiens and Péronne. Though the French had hoped to help, they were so distracted by their efforts at Verdun that the British under General Haig were left to do battle with only minor assistance from the French. Haig carefully planned what he thought would be a devastating attack on the heart of the German line. What he orchestrated instead was the biggest single-day disaster in the history of the British army.

Beginning on June 23, 1916, the British launched what was to be the most sustained artillery attack of the war. Lasting for a week and consuming one and a half million shells, the bombardment could be heard all the way to England. Haig believed such shelling, conducted both wide and deep across German defenses, would thoroughly destroy the German trench system. On July 1, 1916, the bombing stopped and the British soldiers, almost all newly recruited to the army, climbed up out of their trenches to claim their victory. They had been told, according to a source quoted by Winter and Baggett, "You will be able to go over the top with a walking stick, you will not need rifles.... You will find the Germans all dead, not even a rat will have survived."

British private W. Slater, also quoted by Winter and Baggett, recounted what really happened: "For some reason nothing seemed to happen to us at first; we strolled along as though walking in a park. Then, suddenly, we were in the midst of a storm of machine gun bullets and I saw men beginning to twirl round and fall in all kinds of curious ways as they were hit—quite unlike the way actors do it in films." His experience was repeated across the wide front. German soldiers climbed up out of their trenches, manned their machine guns, and raked the lines of men with their withering fire. By the end of that first day's attack, 20,000 British soldiers had been killed, 40,000 wounded. Several brigades lost a majority of their men; the fourteenth platoon of the First Rifle Brigade lost 39 of 40 men. What had happened?

Haig's Mistake

The first day of the Battle of the Somme was an utter disaster for the Allies, but why? The simple answer is the artillery bombardment did not work: German trenches were deeper and stronger than expected and largely survived the days of bombing; German barbed wire, thicker than the kind used by the British, also survived the bombs and couldn't be cut by British wire cutters. When the British marched across what they thought would be an open field, they were slowed by the unbroken barbed wire and then mowed down by unfazed German soldiers. Even when the bombs worked on the first line of trenches, the Germans fell back to a second and third line of trenches.

Undaunted by the first day's disaster—in fact, poor communications meant he didn't even understand it was a disaster—Haig ordered his men to battle on. For days the British threw themselves against the German line. On July 14 they got through the second German line, only to be turned back by fresh German reserves. The Germans then set about to regain the ground they had lost, and the Somme settled into a pattern that was much like Verdun. Through August and September and into the fall, British and German troops took turns trying to break the other. Neither succeeded.

On September 15, Haig ordered a new weapon onto the battlefield: the landship, later called the tank. Though he was not convinced that these armored vehicles equipped with guns would be effective, Haig thought that they couldn't hurt. Forty-nine tanks crawled forward at a pace of half a mile an hour; only eighteen made it as far as no-man's-land. The new vehicles frightened the German soldiers at first but did little other damage; they would be developed further for future battles.

In the end, it was weather and fatigue that brought the Battle of the Somme to a close at the end of November. The British had succeeded in advancing six miles and claiming the village of Beaumont-Hamel; it was a meager prize for such a cost in lives. The British took 420,000 casualties in this battle alone, followed by 195,000 for the French. The Germans sustained a total of 650,000 casualties. In a battle in which all took heavy losses, the British, with their small gain in territory, declared themselves the winner.

Conclusion

By the winter of 1916–17 the combatants had been fighting for more than two whole years, yet little had been decided. For two years, the British, French, and German armies had faced each other across the no-man's-land that lay between their lines of trenches. For two years, the combatants had launched brutal, futile attacks on armies highly skilled in the art of defense. For two years, these countries had sent a generation of men to die in battles that resulted in the gain of a few yards of earth. The soldiers were growing tired; so too were the countries they defended. Yet the war went on. By the winter of 1916–17, however, generals on both sides recognized that things would have to change in the coming year. The entrance of the United States into the war and the withdrawal of Russia would bring changes; advances in technology and changing tactics would also alter the course of the war. But one thing would remain the same: On the Western Front, death would reign supreme.

For More Information

Bosco, Peter. *World War I*. New York: Facts on File, 1991.

Clare, John D., ed. *First World War*. San Diego, CA: Harcourt Brace, 1995.

The Great War and the Shaping of the 20th Century. [Online] http://www.pbs.org/greatwar (accessed October 2000).

Griffiths, Paddy. *Battle Tactics on the Western Front, 1916–1918*. New Haven, CT: Yale University Press, 1994.

Kent, Zachary. *World War I: "The War to End Wars."* Hillside, NJ: Enslow, 1994.

Macdonald, Lyn. *1914–1918: Voices and Images of the Great War*. New York: Penguin Books, 1991.

Sommerville, Donald. *World War I: History of Warfare*. Austin, TX: Raintree Steck-Vaughn, 1999.

Stewart, Gail. *World War One*. San Diego, CA: Lucent, 1991.

World War I: Trenches on the Web. [Online] http://www.worldwar1.com (accessed October 2000).

Sources

Dooly, Jr., William G. *Great Weapons of World War I*. New York: Bonanza Books, 1969.

Gilbert, Martin. *The First World War: A Complete History*. New York: Henry Holt, 1994.

Heyman, Neil M. *World War I*. Westport, CT: Greenwood Press, 1997.

Keegan, John. *The First World War*. New York: Alfred A. Knopf, 1999.

Stokesbury, James L. *A Short History of World War I.* New York: William Morrow, 1981.

Winter, J. M. *The Experience of World War I.* New York: Oxford University Press, 1989.

Winter, Jay, and Blain Baggett. *The Great War and the Shaping of the 20th Century.* New York: Penguin Studio, 1996.

Changing Tides of War on the Western Front

4

By the spring of 1917 World War I had been raging for over two years, yet little had been decided. In the first few months of the war German troops had stormed across Belgium, hoping to win a quick victory over the French. But the Germans had run into the determined resistance of British, French, and Belgian troops—known as the Allies—along a long line known as the Western Front (which stretched 475 miles across Europe from the North Sea in Belgium southeast to the border of neutral Switzerland). For two years, these bitter enemies had fought fiercely in battles that claimed many, many lives but little territory. Soldiers on both sides wondered what the new year of war would bring. Would there be more death and destruction as men fell to the killing power of machine-guns, artillery, and poison gas? Or would their leaders devise some new way to win a war that many people thought was now not winnable?

Behind the lines, politicians and generals looked for ways to break out of the habits that had led to a war of stalemate. Both Britain and France experienced major changes in leadership. British prime minister Herbert Asquith (1852–1928),

Poisonous gases acted immediately on soldiers who weren't properly protected. *Reproduced by permission of Corbis Corporation (Bellevue).*

who had left the war effort largely to the generals, resigned and was replaced on December 1, 1916, by David Lloyd George (1863–1945). In France, Commander in Chief Joseph Joffre (1852–1931)—who directed assaults on the German line that cost hundreds of thousands of French casualties—was replaced by General Robert Nivelle (1857–1924). Nivelle proposed a strategy that must have seemed familiar to soldiers who had served during the first two years of the war under Joffre: the French would go on the offensive.

A major assault in the central area of the Western Front, near the River Aisne, was planned. The French hoped to split the German line in two and cut off the German troops to the northwest. Carrying out this plan would nearly destroy the French army. The British would try once again to triumph over the Germans near Ypres (pronounced ee-per); if they succeeded, they would flank the Germans and surround them from the northwest. As in previous battles, both the French and the British planned to launch attacks with artillery bombardment and then follow the bombing with a massive push from the infantry.

For their part, the Germans were ever more committed to waging a war of defense. They were on the verge of ending the war with the Russians on the Eastern Front. If Germany could just hold out a bit longer on the Western Front, it would soon have reinforcements from the east. The Germans made their defenses even stronger on the Western Front, establishing second and third rows of trenches in many places. About twenty-five miles behind the westernmost bulge in the front, the Germans constructed massive new defensive fortifications that they called the Siegfried Zone; the Allies called it the Hindenburg line. As the Germans withdrew to this new defensive line, they destroyed everything in their path—roads, bridges, railways, towns—making it all the more difficult for the Allies to advance.

The Battle of the Aisne

The French began the Second Battle of the Aisne (also known as the Nivelle offensive) with an enthusiasm they had not felt in many months. Their new commander, Robert Nivelle, was optimistic, and he conveyed his enthusiasm to the soldiers. He told his men that they would "rupture" the German defense. General E. L. Spears, a British officer viewing troop preparations, described the scene, as quoted in John Keegan's *The First World War:* "A thrill of something like pleasure . . . ran through the troops. I was surrounded by the grinning faces of men whose eyes shone . . . . The effect of the cheerful voices was enhanced by the sparkles of light dancing on thousands of blue steel helmets." In all, some 1,200,000 soldiers prepared to support this important battle.

On April 16, the attack started; like so many others, it began with a solid day of artillery bombardment. As the bombing shifted to further back in the German line, the French infantry pressed forward in great numbers. They broke through quickly— too quickly— and began to advance. Then the tide began to shift. German airplanes dominated the skies and informed the German artillery of the location of French troops; the German gunners rained bombs down on the advancing men. The Germans had intentionally made their

first line of defense weak; the real strength of their defense lay in the second and third lines. By the time the exhausted French soldiers had pressed that far forward, they faced fresh German troops—and snarling machine guns.

The French were taking a beating, but they pressed on for two, three, four days. According to Keegan, "On the first day [the French] penetrated no more than 600 yards; on the third day the Chemins des Dames road, crossing the ridge, was reached; on the fifth day, when 130,000 casualties had been suffered, the offensive was effectively abandoned. There had been compensatory gains, including 28,815 prisoners, and a penetration of four miles on a sixteen mile front, but the deep German defenses remained intact." Nivelle did not want to face the fact that a French offensive had once again failed to break the solid German line. In fact, instead of breaking the German line, the attack at Aisne had come close to breaking the French army.

Mutiny in the French Army

As the Nivelle offensive faltered, ordinary French soldiers began to revolt against the war effort. These soldiers had long been underpaid, underfed, and forced to live in impossible conditions. For over two years they had obediently trudged forth to fight the generals' battles, but now they no longer had any faith that their generals were sending them into battles they could win. According to Stokesbury, "Reinforcements going up to the line [in the Battle of the Aisne] were sullen and slow. Passing their generals they baa-ed, imitating the noises of sheep being led to a slaughterhouse." As the Nivelle offensive failed, these men refused to fight any longer.

Historians have called these actions the "mutinies of 1917," but this overstates what actually happened. Soldiers did not desert the army or attack their officers. Instead, in great numbers—some estimates suggest that 500,000 soldiers were involved—they simply refused to attack the German lines. These soldiers would defend their soil, but they wanted leave to visit their families, more and better food, and better medical care. They wanted to be treated like men, not as fodder for German guns.

French politicians wisely sacked Nivelle and brought in the one man who was capable of salvaging the French army: Philippe Pétain (1856–1951). Pétain was beloved by the soldiers. He seemed to understand the difficulties that they faced, and he was known for not wasting French lives in futile assaults. Pétain quickly contained the crisis. He ordered immediate improvements in conditions for soldiers, but he also ordered disciplinary action against the most aggressive of the "mutineers." Fifty-five soldiers were executed for crimes related to their protests, and many more were charged with minor offenses. Though Pétain kept the French army from falling apart, he recognized that there would be no more massive assaults from his army, at least not until the Americans—who had recently declared war on Germany—joined the battle. Luckily, the Germans never learned of the difficulties in the French army, for they surely would have attacked if they had known about the crisis in the French soldiers' morale.

Rare Victories

While the French were preparing for their attack near the River Aisne, the Canadian First Army achieved something quite rare on the Western Front: a clear-cut victory. The Battle of Arras was first conceived as a diversion—it was designed to distract the Germans from the coming attack on the Aisne. The British and Canadians were to take Vimy Ridge, a line of high ground that the French had failed to capture in two previous battles. Surprisingly, the Canadians laid down such an effective artillery barrage that they actually shattered the first German line. Canadian troops commanded by General Julian Byng (1862–1935) quickly broke through and drove the Germans from positions they had maintained for two and a half years. By the end of the day on April 9, Canadian troops stood atop Vimy Ridge and looked eastward over the German defenses. Though they would go no further, this victory was the high point of the war for previously untested Canadian forces. "It is not too imaginative," writes Stokesbury, "to say that Canada became a nation on the slopes of Vimy Ridge."

The Canadians were not the only ones to achieve success in 1917. As part of the preparation for a larger attack near the village of Ypres, British general Herbert "Daddy" Plumer (1857–1932) was charged with taking a German salient, or bulge, that protruded into the Allied line south of Ypres. Using the skills of soldiers who had been coal miners before the war, he ordered his troops to dig long tunnels reaching to beneath the enemy lines. The tunnels were packed with high explosives, and when they were set off on June 7, the huge blast decimated the German line, knocked British soldiers off their feet, and was thought to be an earthquake by people twenty-five miles away. Completely surprising the Germans, the British soldiers quickly pushed past the German line of defense and captured the entire bulge.

Passchendaele: The Third Battle of Ypres

British general Douglas Haig took the Battle of Arras and the capture of the German salient as good omens for his coming attack on the familiar battlefield of Ypres. Once more in 1917 the British would attack the Germans near the town of Ypres, where the British had already been involved in two bloody, fruitless battles (See Chapter 3); this time, thought Haig, they would use their artillery fire better, have better-rested and better-supplied men, and somehow crash through the German line. The artillery bombardment began as scheduled on July 18 and continued for thirteen days before soldiers began climbing up out of their trenches to face the Germans directly on July 31. The British advanced two miles that first day, pushing forward into German defenses weakened by the shelling. And then the rains came.

The area around Ypres was low and wet even in good weather conditions, but the rain that began to fall on August 1 soon saturated the soil. The shelling had turned this the soft, wet soil into a morass of water-filled craters, a sea of mud. Furthermore, it had destroyed the carefully constructed drainage system that offered the one hope of keeping the area passable. Soon the British soldiers found themselves struggling just to move. Men, horses, and trucks became stuck in the mud; the trenches in which men tried to take refuge filled with water. Soldiers wounded in battle drowned in the water-filled craters. Haig, unwilling to halt an offensive on which he had gambled so much, ordered more men into the muddy field. The Germans, with their better-constructed trenches, remained in command, slaughtering their struggling opponents even as the British retreated.

For weeks Haig sent his troops forward. They measured their gains in yards, not the miles Haig had hoped for. Young British officer Edward Campion Vaughan described the conditions on the field of battle in his diary, as quoted in Winter and Baggett's *The Great War:*

> *From the darkness on all sides came the groans and wails of wounded men; faint, long, sobbing moans of agony, and despairing shrieks. It was too horribly obvious that dozens of men with serious wounds must have crawled for safety into new shell-holes, and now the water was rising about them and, powerless to move, they were slowly drowning. Horrible visions came to me with those cries—of Woods and Ken, Edge and Taylor, lying maimed out there trusting that their pals*

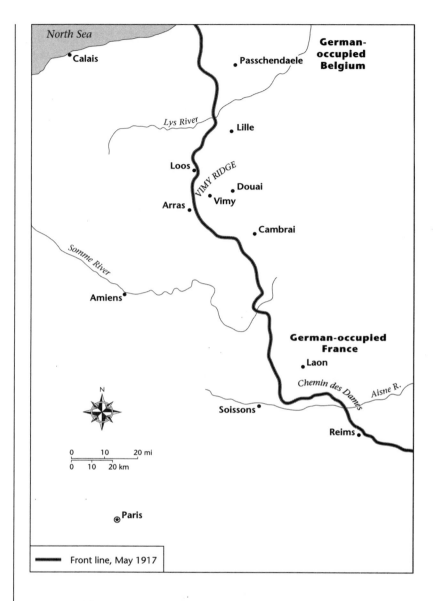

North Sea
German-occupied Belgium
Calais
Passchendaele
Lys River
Lille
Loos
VIMY RIDGE
Douai
Vimy
Arras
Cambrai
Somme River
Amiens
German-occupied France
Laon
Chemin des Dames
Aisne R.
Soissons
Reims
N
0 10 20 mi
0 10 20 km
Paris
——— Front line, May 1917

would find them, and now dying terribly, alone amongst the dead in the inky darkness. And we could do nothing to help them.

Finally, after weeks of battle, Canadians involved in the attack took the village of Passchendaele and Haig saw fit to declare victory and end the battle. It was November 10; the British had gained just over four miles of territory at the cost of some 250,000 casualties.

Passchendaele pointed out to everyone involved the folly of continuing the massive attacks on heavily fortified German lines. British soldiers, once known for their enthusiasm in fighting for their country, seemed suddenly weary and shell-shocked. And for the first time, their officers became aware of the carnage that they had ordered their men into. In *A Short History of World War I,* James Stokesbury recounts the story of a British officer who surveyed the battlefield after the fighting: "He gazed out over the sea of mud, then said half to himself, 'My God, did we send men to advance in that?' after which he broke down weeping and his escort led him away." Just as the Nivelle offensive had thrown the French army into disarray, Passchendaele made many in the British army wonder how they could go on.

A New Way of Waging War

The Nivelle offensive and the Battle of Passchendaele were "old-style" battles, battles begun with artillery bombardments and fought by infantry charging across no-man's-land to take on the enemy. But by the fall of 1917, the Western Front was seeing the first of the new ways of conducting war.

Tanks had been used in battle before—by the British at the Battle of the Somme and by the French in the Nivelle offensive—but they had proved of little use. By November 1917, however, the British had made such improvements in the tanks' construction that these vehicles could now make a difference. The new British tanks, with their heavy armor and Caterpillar treads, could cross difficult terrain and launch a powerful attack. Better still, they did not need to have the way cleared by artillery barrage. On November 20, the British committed their entire Tank Corps to an assault on the Germans in the Battle of Cambrai.

Tanks and infantry advanced together. Over three hundred tanks smashed through the German barbed wire and crossed German trenches. The infantry followed close behind. Many Germans panicked at the sight of the gigantic metal monsters coming toward them and threw down their guns and ran. The British quickly gained ground, and for a time it looked like they would clear the field of Germans. Only a shortage of reinforcements kept the British from claiming more ground. The Battle of Cambrai proved the war-worthiness of the tank and showed that attacks could be effective without artillery support.

British tank *Winston's Folly* going over a trench.
Reproduced by permission of Corbis Corporation (Bellevue).

No sooner had the British called off their attack, however, than the Germans won a small victory using new techniques of their own. Borrowing from tactics developed on the Eastern Front and in fighting in Italy, the Germans launched a speedy surprise attack on the same ground the British had just gained. Grouped in small squadrons and unsupported by artillery shelling, the Germans quickly pushed the British back. Within a few days they had returned the front line roughly to the position it had been before the tank attack. Though neither the British tank attack nor the German surprise attack was decisive, both events indicated the shape of battles to come.

The Waiting Game: Preparing for the End

As 1917 came to a close, leaders on both sides recognized that the year to come might well bring the end of the war. How the war would end, however, was very much in doubt. For more than three years, Allied forces and soldiers representing the Central Powers had fought to a standstill on the Western Front. Despite their best efforts, neither side was capable of inflicting enough damage on the other to force a collapse. But leaders awaited a shift of power that might tip the delicate balance.

For Germany, the waiting game had the air of desperation. Simply put, Germany could not afford to wage war for too much longer. It had called forth nearly all of its manpower and resources to wage war, and now the nation was quite literally starving to death. An Allied blockade kept supplies from reaching Germany, and the nation's farms were no longer capable of meeting the demand for food. If Germany was to win the war, it needed to win the war soon. With this in mind, generals on the Western Front awaited the arrival of reinforcements from the east, where Russia had been defeated. These reinforcements would provide the manpower for one final offensive, which was to be launched in the spring, before the American troops that were streaming into France could be prepared for fighting. German military leader Ludendorff, who masterminded what has become known as the "spring offensive," hoped that the Germans could use these reinforcements to finally bring the Allies to their knees.

France and Britain played a waiting game of their own: They waited for the Americans. When the United States entered the war on April 6, 1917, France and Britain looked forward to using American manpower to help win the war. But the American troops were slow in coming, and their leader, General John Pershing (1860–1948), refused to allow his men

to serve under non-American generals. Still, by March 1918 there were 325,000 Americans in France, and their mere presence was a source of moral support for the Allies.

German Spring Offensives

Ludendorff knew of the arrival of the Americans, and he knew that if he would have victory, he must have it in the spring. As he had before, Ludendorff decided to attack at the point where the British and French forces met, near the Somme River. The major German attack would concentrate on routing the British and driving them northward; a secondary assault would split the British and French lines and seal the French to the south, where they could no longer come to the rescue of the British.

The German spring offensive began on March 21, 1918. In the usual way, first came the artillery barrage, next the poison gas, and finally the charge of the infantry. With their careful planning, the Germans' charge was highly effective. They broke through the British and French lines, driving the Allies to the rear. It was the most wide-open battle the Western Front had seen in years. The German push through the French line to the south was so successful that Ludendorff decided to keep driving forward, hoping to take the French town of Amiens.

Ferdinand Foch. *Reproduced courtesy of the Library of Congress.*

This German charge threw the Allies into disarray. The Allied leaders met to decide how to resist the attack. Fearing that the Germans might succeed in splitting the French and British forces, the Allies agreed to coordinate their efforts under the command of French general Ferdinand Foch (1851–1929). Working together, the British and French defenses stiffened and finally stopped the German attack on April 4. The Germans could not have carried the battle much further anyway, because they did not have the capacity to ship men and supplies much further forward. For the Allies, much had been lost: The Germans had driven them back nearly forty miles, taking territory that Germany had not held since the early days of the war.

Cheered by the success, Ludendorff attacked again, hoping to destroy the British will to fight. This attack, known as the Battle of Lys, came just south of the familiar

The Shelling of Paris

While German land forces were launching their final attacks on the British and French troops along the Western Front in the spring of 1918, the German artillery was unleashing a new and horrifying weapon on the heart of the French nation, the city of Paris. From positions in the forests near Laon, about seventy miles from the city, German gunners fired the most powerful guns ever used in warfare.

These big German artillery guns were not efficient—they could only fire sixty-five shells before they had to be retooled—but they were formidable: "Fired at a steep angle into the air, the shells rose to a height of twenty-four miles before descending, and they took nearly three minutes to reach their target," writes historian James Stokesbury. From March 23 to April 9, the Germans fired nearly four hundred shells on Paris, causing almost nine hundred casualties in the city. The most dramatic attack, which occurred on Good Friday, March 29, smashed into the Church of St. Gervais.

Despite the costs of his victories, Germany's Ludendorff pushed on. His next point of attack was on the French troops positioned near another familiar battlefield, the Chemin des Dames. The effective quick-strike tactics of the Germans combined with an unfortunate concentration of French forces right at the point of the heaviest battlefield of Ypres. Fourteen German divisions smashed into the British line and soon overwhelmed the British as well as a Portuguese division that had been sent into battle. The Germans released over two thousand tons of poison gas, including mustard gas, phosgene, and diphenylchlorarsine, according to Martin Gilbert, "incapacitating 8,000 men, of whom many were blinded, and killing thirty." The battle was going so badly for the British that General Douglas Haig issued a rare rallying call to his troops, quoted in Stokesbury's *Short History of World War I:* "With our backs to the wall and believing in the justice of our cause each one must fight to the end. The safety of our homes and the freedom of mankind alike depend upon the conduct of each one of us at this critical moment." These words reveal how desperate the situation seemed for the Allies.

German shelling gave the Germans a major victory. Overrunning the French front lines, the Germans pushed forward thirteen miles in a single day, May 27, and kept moving from there. Despite resistance from retreating French troops, the Germans pushed on for a week, until they reached the Marne River. They were now within forty miles of Paris, but that was as close as they would get.

The German advance southward stalled for all the old reasons, plus one new one. As in previous battles fought on the Western Front, retreating armies had an advantage once they got organized. French troops fell back to strong positions and rained fire on the advancing German troops, making them pay for whatever ground they gained. And German supply lines simply couldn't keep up with the pace of the advancing army. German troops pushing forward had to stop to await fresh food and ammunition. Finally, German troops met up with the one force that was to change the tide of the battle: American soldiers. Untested as they were, these American troops were well-supplied and eager for battle. The German troops facing the Americans were surprised at how fresh and strong the American troops were. In many places, the German advance stopped when it met the American line.

Though the Battle of Lys went well for the Germans—they succeeded in pushing the British back several miles—it did not go well enough. The British defenses stiffened and held their ground, and the Germans lost thirty thousand casualties to the Allies' twenty thousand. Even worse, perhaps, was the effect that the battle had on the Germans' morale. German soldiers fresh from the Eastern Front had been told that they would walk right over the British; instead, they were met with firm resistance and suffered heavy casualties. Furthermore, writes Stokesbury, "When [German soldiers] got into British rear areas, [they] were astounded and appalled by the wealth of [military supplies], rations, clothes, and general sense of well-being that they found." The British were much better supplied than the Germans, who were nearing starvation behind their lines, and many German soldiers felt that there was no way such an enemy could be defeated.

British officer leading raiding party out of the trenches to harass the German lines. *Reproduced by permission of Archive Photos, Inc.*

The Collapse of the Spring Offensive

Ludendorff was claiming small victories, but he was not winning the war. In fact, he had lost nearly 600,000 casualties in his three victories so far, with increasing numbers of the casualties consisting of troops that either deserted or gave themselves up to Allied forces. Convinced that he still might break through if he kept on trying, Ludendorff planned two final assaults, the fourth and fifth attacks of the Germans' spring offensive. The fourth attack was to begin on June 9 on a front nearly twenty miles long, stretching from Montdidier to Noyon. But French troops had learned of the assault from German deserters and surprised the German soldiers by beginning their shelling just before the Germans could begin theirs. Though confused by this setback, the German attack still managed to gain several miles of ground before stalling against the combined might of the French and American defenses. With casualties mounting, the attack was called off within a matter of days.

The fifth and final German offensive action was doomed from the outset. The French had learned many of the details of the attack from the steady stream of German deserters crossing over to the west. The deserters revealed that the Germans planned an artillery attack near the city of Reims, to be followed by an infantry advance. Once again, the French artillery barrage began first, and the French mounted an effective counterattack that came just after the Germans' first attack wave faltered. All over the Allied line, French, British, American, and Italian troops fought with great determination. Surrounded on three sides, one American division still managed to hold its position; one of its regiments earned the nickname "the Rock of the Marne." On July 18, just days after the battle began, the Germans halted their attack. By July 22 they were in full retreat and were giving up ground that they had recently captured. The German assault had ended.

Hearing of these setbacks, German chancellor Georg von Hertling wrote, according to Gilbert, "On the 18th even the most optimistic among us knew that all was lost. The history of the world was played out in three days." Across the German front that feeling was shared. German troops retreating from battle met their reinforcements—still coming forward—with scorn, wondering how these men could continue to support what was clearly a lost cause. Even Ludendorff and Hindenburg, the architects of Germany's years-long war effort, were despondent. According to Stokesbury, Ludendorff went to see Hindenburg and asked him what Germany ought to do now. "Do? Do!" Hindenburg bellowed. "Make peace, you idiot!" But it was not that easy. German leaders wanted to be sure they argued from a position of power in any peace negotiations. To do so, they would have to hold their ground on the Western Front and convince the Allies that Germany was an equal in power and not a defeated nation. Ludendorff's words, quoted by Gilbert, summarized Germany's position: "We cannot win this war any more, but we must not lose it." And so, in order to try to win the peace, the exhausted German army battled into the fall trying hard not to lose the war.

The Allied Offensive

On the day the final German offensive faltered, July 18, 1918, the Allies began what was to be the final stage of the

German spring offensives, Hindenburg Line, and areas of conquest from March–July 1918.

Reproduced by permission of The Gale Group.

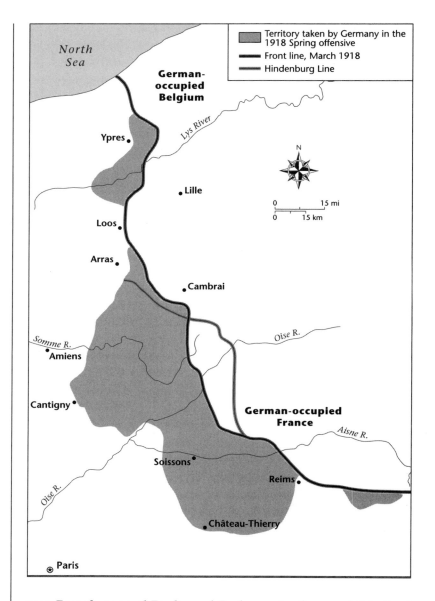

Territory taken by Germany in the 1918 Spring offensive
Front line, March 1918
Hindenburg Line

North Sea

German-occupied Belgium

Ypres

Lys River

Lille

Loos

Arras

Cambrai

Oise R.

Somme R.

Amiens

Cantigny

German-occupied France

Aisne R.

Soissons

Reims

Oise R.

Château-Thierry

Paris

war. French general Ferdinand Foch was in charge of this final Allied offensive, and he commanded not only the experienced armies of French and British soldiers but also the fresh American forces led by General Pershing. (The Allies had agreed to coordinate their efforts under French command, though Americans were still commanded by American officers in battle.) Near the Marne, French, British, Italian, and American troops worked together in the slow process of driving the Germans backward into submission. In the first phase of this attack nearly three hundred French tanks were used to cross German trenches and wipe out machine-gun nests. Many of the American troops got their first taste of battle in this encounter, though it was against German troops ravaged by fatigue and falling back in retreat. By August 3 the Allies had achieved their objective of pushing back the bulge that the Germans had created in the line.

Shattering the German Line

The first phase of the Allied offensive worked well, but the second proved devastating to the Germans. The site of the Germans' furthest westward advance was a huge salient that reached nearly to the French city of Amiens; it was here that the Allies massed an overwhelming force that included twenty-seven infantry divisions, more than six hundred tanks, nearly two thousand aircraft, and masses of artillery. To defend themselves the Germans had only twenty divisions of men, and these were racked by desertions and fatigue. On August 8 the Allies began pushing forward at great speed. Within a day they had driven some of the Germans out of their trenches and broken out into the rear of the front. Suddenly a battlefront that had seemed impenetrable was open, and the Allies were on the move.

For the Germans, August 8 was the worst day of a long and terrible war. On that day, a Canadian division took twelve villages and five thousand German prisoners; not to be outdone, Australians captured seven villages and eight thousand prisoners of their own. It got worse for the Germans. On August 10, twenty-four thousand more Germans were taken prisoner. Many German soldiers simply surrendered to the enemy at the first opportunity. In some areas, German officers ordered their men forward at gunpoint. And yet, despite this collapse, some German units did manage to put up resistance.

The U.S. First Army's First Victory

The Allied drive continued forward across a wide front, and the Allies quickly regained all the ground that the Germans had taken in the spring offensive. The Americans too had their first major success to the southeast. On the far-

Men in Charge: Erich Ludendorff

The most powerful leader in Germany was neither Kaiser Wilhelm nor Field Marshal Paul von Hindenburg, but rather Hindenburg's assistant—Erich Ludendorff (1865–1937). During the last few years of the war, Ludendorff was, in the words of World War I author Neil M. Heyman, "virtual dictator over the affairs of his country."

Born on April 9, 1865, Ludendorff became a career military officer. After attending the German General Staff Academy (a military training school), he occupied several key positions during peacetime. Ludendorff first gained notice as a military commander when he led the assault on the Belgian fortress city of Liège in the first battle of World War I. He attained real power as chief of staff of the German Eighth Army on the Eastern Front. Teamed with Hindenburg, Ludendorff helped Germany dominate the Eastern Front. In 1916, when General Erich von Falkenhayn was relieved of his command, Hindenburg and Ludendorff took charge of the German military.

As first quartermaster general to Hindenburg's chief of the general staff, Ludendorff called the shots in the major decisions about the German military. He backed better offensive tactics, stronger defensive positions, unrestricted submarine warfare, and the drafting of all able German males into the military. It was Ludendorff who masterminded the German "spring offensive" of 1918. Ludendorff struggled to hold the German military together as the Central Powers collapsed late in 1918, and he resigned in October of that year. After the war, Ludendorff backed Nazi leader Adolf Hitler before fading from public life and dying in 1937.

eastern end of the Western Front, the Americans had finally organized themselves into the U.S. First Army. Their task would be to retake what was known as the Saint-Mihiel salient, a narrow triangular bulge that stretched into Allied territory. On September 12, two hundred thousand American troops supported by forty-eight thousand French troops began their attack. They were aided by the use of thousands of shells of phosgene gas and by the support of nearly fifteen hundred airplanes, the heaviest concentration of air support yet seen in the war.

The American-led attack came at the worst possible time for the Germans, who had begun retreating to stronger defensive positions on September 11. U.S. general Pershing wanted a quick advance and that was what he got: Within twelve hours the Americans had pushed the Germans back nearly fifteen miles. Within forty-eight hours they had pushed the Germans all the way out of the salient and taken fifteen thousand prisoners and two hundred fifty heavy guns as well. The story of American soldier Sergeant Harry J. Adams, recounted by Martin Gilbert in *The First World War,* captures the essence of the American victory: Adams approached a German dugout (a room dug into the earth) with only two bullets remaining in his gun. Thinking there were just a few soldiers inside, he rushed in, fired his two bullets, and demanded that the Germans surrender. To his astonishment, German soldiers poured forth from their earthen bunker—there were 300 in all. The single American soldier marched his captives back to the American line.

Not every encounter went so well for the Americans. In all, more than four thousand Americans were killed in the taking of the Saint-Mihiel salient. But the Americans proved to their allies and to the Germans that they were a force to be reckoned with. A British newspaper, the *Manchester Guardian,* summed up the victory (as quoted in Gilbert): "It is as swift and neat an operation as any in the war, and perhaps the most heartening of all its features is the proof it gives that the precision, skills, and imagination of American leadership is not inferior to the spirit of their troops."

Through August and September the Allies achieved success after success. They drove the Germans back out of the three blocks of territory that the German soldiers had captured in the spring, and Allied troops now stood poised to attack at points all along the Western Front. Leaders and generals who once feared that the war must go on into 1919 began to make plans to finish the affair before the end of the year. Ferdinand Foch's plan was to alternate his attack at four points, in order to exhaust the German reserves as German soldiers moved from one point to another. With superior numbers of men, guns, tanks, and planes, and with troop confidence higher than it had been in years, the Allies seemed poised to rout their enemy. They did not quite do that, for the Germans still had some fight left in them.

Limy, through which American forces passed in cutting off the Saint-Mihiel salient. *Reproduced courtesy of the Library of Congress.*

The Battle of the Meuse-Argonne

The final Allied offensive began at the Battle of the Meuse-Argonne. The Meuse River flowed south into France from Belgium and was flanked on the west by the Argonne Forest, a dense tangle of trees and hills. If the Allies could drive the Germans out of this area, they could close off the rail lines that transported supplies from the east to German troops in the west. It was a strategically important area, and the Germans were not about to give it up easily.

On the night of September 25 combined French and American forces began their bombardment of German positions in the Meuse-Argonne region. Their gas attacks alone debilitated about ten thousand German troops, and on September 26 and 27 they advanced toward the German lines behind a line of tanks. By the evening of September 27 the Allies had crawled forward six miles, but their progress soon slowed. By September 29 the Allies stopped dead against strong German defensive positions in the Argonne Forest.

Men in Charge: Ferdinand Foch

Though France had many generals during World War I, the one who received perhaps the most credit for the final Allied victory was General Ferdinand Foch (1851–1929). Taking charge after the brutal German spring offensive of 1918, Foch (pronounced "Fawsh") coordinated the efforts of British, American, French, and other Allied forces in the final offensive that led to German surrender.

Born on October 2, 1851, Foch already had a distinguished military career before the start of World War I. He had served as an officer, taught at and eventually directed the École Supérieure de la Guerre (War School), and published two influential books on military techniques. Early in the war Foch had success as commander of the French Ninth Army in the Battle of the Marne, which took place in September 1914. As with other generals who achieved success early, however, the sheer cost of waging war on the Western

Front eventually counted against Foch. When he lost numbers of troops during the Battle of the Somme in 1916, he was removed from command.

Foch returned to power in 1917 as chief of the French general staff, a noncombat position. He oversaw successful operations in Italy and was well liked by politicians. When the German spring offensive of 1918 took its toll on French confidence, Foch was placed in charge. He rallied British and American generals to carry out his plan for a concentrated offensive all along the Western Front, and he oversaw the successful Allied effort that ended the war. Foch convinced the politicians who were in charge of making peace to strip the German army of its ability to fight, but he could not convince them to take large chunks of German territory. Foch retired a hero and died in Paris in 1929.

Despite throwing waves of attackers forward, the Allies could not root out the Germans from their positions among the rocks and trees of the Argonne.

For ten days the Americans kept pouring men into the Argonne woods. Their losses were heavy, but unlike the other combatants they were able to bring fresh reinforcements and plentiful supplies to the line. It was in the battle for the Argonne Forest that the American "Lost Battalion" became famous. Separated from their retreating battalions, a band of American soldiers found themselves deep in enemy territory,

American soldiers escorting German prisoners to the rear during the battle of the Argonne in France.
Reproduced courtesy of the Library of Congress.

surrounded by Germans and given up for lost by American commanders. According to Stokesbury, "The remnants of two battalions hunkered down in a ravine, fighting off Germans from all sides and dodging barrages of grenades lobbed down the slopes at them. After five days the Germans sent them a very courteous letter suggesting they surrender, to which the response was a profane chorus of 'Come and get us!'" Finally, on October 8, American troops pushing forward drove the Germans away, and the "Lost Battalion" was found. By October 10 the Americans had finally cleared the Argonne Forest, but at a far greater cost in lives than they had anticipated.

To the north and west another battle was raging. British troops led by General Douglas Haig attacked a long front between the French towns of Arras and Cambrai. The battle had begun on September 28, and now, finally, British troops achieved the kinds of successes that had eluded them for years. The Germans had already begun to withdraw when the Allied attacks came on. Day after day for three weeks the

British ground forward, taking towns that had been under German control since the beginning of the war, and capturing huge numbers of German soldiers. Casualties were heavy on both sides, but the momentum was clearly on the side of the Allies. Early in October the Allies crashed through a thirty-mile stretch of the Hindenburg line east of Arras.

Soldiers of the American 23rd Infantry of the Second Division U.S. Army lying on the ground and firing a 37mm gun at the German position in the Argonne. *Reproduced by permission of Archive Photos, Inc.*

The Central Powers Collapse

By mid-October everything on the Western Front had changed. Within Germany both soldiers and politicians recognized that the war was lost, and on October 11 German forces began a systematic withdrawal from the Western Front. Battles continued all along the line: British, French, American, Canadian, and Australian troops pushed forward, liberating town after town from German rule; German soldiers fought desperately in retreat. The best the Germans could hope for at this point was to stop the Allies before they entered Germany itself,

Ruins of houses destroyed in the last zeppelin bombing raid in Paris, France.
Reproduced by permission of Corbis Corporation (Bellevue).

or to slow them up enough that winter would bring an end to the hostilities. Even as the fighting raged on, however, the decisions of political leaders and generals in faraway cities and on faraway fronts were bringing World War I to a close. Two things especially helped bring the end of the war: the collapse of Germany's allies and the disintegration of Germany's leadership.

Bulgaria became the first of the Central Powers to surrender when it signed an armistice (truce) on September 29. This agreement allowed Allied troops to enter the Balkan region, within striking distance of Germany's southeastern border. Turkey followed signed its armistice a month later on October 30. Among the conditions of the truce was that Turkey must allow Allied troops to occupy the country for military purposes. The noose was thus tightened further on Germany. Soon Austria-Hungary, Germany's closest ally and once its most powerful partner, ended its war efforts as well. The stress of war had caused widespread dissension among the many peoples that made up the Austro-Hungarian Empire.

Poles, Czechs, Yugoslavs, and Romanians within Austria-Hungary all longed for their independence, and their demands began to tear the empire apart in October of 1918. By October 29 Austria and Hungary seceded from their own empire. Remnant members of the imperial government signed a truce with the Allies on November 3.

Without allies, Germany had good reason to wonder how it could go on fighting with what seemed like the entire world aligned against it. The political leadership of Germany had been in disarray since July 1917, when Chancellor Bethmann Hollweg had resigned and been replaced by a string of leaders more interested in pleasing the military than the nation's people. As long as the politicians and the generals acted together, Germany was able to continue waging war, but this cooperation ended when Maximilian (1867-1929; known as the Prince of Baden) became chancellor on October 4, 1918. When he began to appeal to American president Woodrow Wilson to negotiate for peace, it was truly the beginning of the end for Germany.

Unwilling to go on without political support, Erich Ludendorff resigned from his position as co-commander of the German army on October 26. While Chancellor Maximilian continued negotiations with President Wilson, Germany began to disintegrate around him. The German navy mutinied when asked to take to the sea for one final battle. Throughout the country, people rioted in the streets in a full-scale revolution. They demanded the end of the war and called for the kaiser to abdicate, or give up the throne. Soldiers began leaving their posts or ignoring the commands of their officers. On November 8 Kaiser Wilhelm abdicated the throne and moved to Holland, where he lived the rest of his life in exile (forced removal from his own country).

On November 9 Germany became a republic—which meant that its political leader was no longer appointed by the Kaiser but instead was chosen by the parliament, which represented the people—as Chancellor Maximilian surrendered power to a party called the Social Democrats. The first act of the new German government was to seek peace. The Allied demands were harsh: Germany must withdraw its troops across the wide Western Front, and it must surrender massive numbers of trucks, rail equipment, submarines, and guns. In short, the Germans had to render themselves incapable of waging war. On November 11 the German government signed the armistice agreement. The war was over.

For More Information

Bosco, Peter. *World War I*. New York: Facts on File, 1991.

Clare, John D., ed. *First World War*. San Diego, CA: Harcourt Brace, 1995.

"The Great War and the Shaping of the 20th Century." [Online] http://www.pbs.org/greatwar (accessed October 2000).

Griffiths, Paddy. *Battle Tactics on the Western Front, 1916–1918*. New Haven, CT: Yale University Press, 1994.

Kent, Zachary. *World War I: "The War to End Wars."* Hillside, NJ: Enslow, 1994.

Macdonald, Lyn. *1914–1918: Voices and Images of the Great War*. New York: Penguin Books, 1991.

Sommerville, Donald. *World War I: History of Warfare*. Austin, TX: Raintree Steck-Vaughn, 1999.

Stewart, Gail. *World War One*. San Diego, CA: Lucent, 1991.

"World War I: Trenches on the Web." [Online] http://www.worldwar1.com (accessed October 2000).

Sources

Gilbert, Martin. *The First World War: A Complete History*. New York: Henry Holt, 1994.

Heyman, Neil M. *World War I*. Westport, CT: Greenwood Press, 1997.

Keegan, John. *The First World War*. New York: Alfred A. Knopf, 1999.

Stokesbury, James L. *A Short History of World War I*. New York: William Morrow, 1981.

Winter, J. M. *The Experience of World War I*. New York: Oxford University Press, 1989.

Winter, Jay, and Blaine Baggett. *The Great War and the Shaping of the 20th Century*. New York: Penguin Studio, 1996.

The War in the East

5

World War I opened in the east as it did in the west: with massive mobilizations of men and matériel (military supplies, including guns and ammunition). The Russians, with their massive population, had millions of men in their army, but it was widely believed that Russia would be slow in getting its soldiers ready for battle. In fact, the German war plan—called the Schlieffen plan—counted on Russian sloth. The Germans expected that they could concentrate on defeating the French in the west before turning their attention eastward to the Russians. Surprisingly speedy Russian mobilization made this impossible and nearly cost Germany the territory of East Prussia. But Russian military organization and efficiency never compared to that of the Germans, and in a little over two years of warfare, the Germans had pushed Russia to the brink of defeat.

While Germany and Russia clashed in the northern half of the Eastern Front, Austria-Hungary fought a two-front war in the south. Austria-Hungary's primary concern was the border it shared with the Russian Empire; this border stretched east to west in a region known as Galicia. Russian assaults early in the war pushed Austria-Hungary back in this area, but with

German support Austria-Hungary eventually regained all of the lost territory. In addition to Russia, Austria-Hungary had to deal with Serbia to its southeast, with Italy to its south, and later in the war with actions in Bulgaria and Romania. The difficulties of fighting so many opponents eventually brought about the destruction of the Austro-Hungarian Empire.

The Eastern Front was very different from the Western Front. On the Western Front, a clearly defined line stretching more than four hundred miles from Switzerland to the Belgian coast separated the warring armies of Germany from those of France, Belgium, and Britain. The Eastern Front was much larger and much less clearly defined. It stretched in a shifting line from the Baltic Sea south and very slightly east to Romania (and later all the way to the Romanian coast on the Black Sea). Nearly a thousand miles long, the Eastern Front crossed through Austria-Hungary and the German state of East Prussia; it had stages in the Russian provinces of Poland and Lithuania as well as in Russia itself. War on the Eastern Front never settled down into trench warfare as it did on the Western Front. Instead, the Eastern Front shifted rapidly as advancing armies made strong offensive pushes and losing armies retreated quickly instead of digging defensive trenches.

Russia Takes the Offensive

Though Germany began the military action in World War I with its advance across Belgium early in August 1914, Russia soon showed that it was capable of launching an offensive as well. The Russian army was full of contradictions: Its men were known throughout the world as some of the toughest, most determined fighters; yet its leadership was deeply troubled. Generals were divided into different political camps and often refused to speak to each other. Russian military tactics were outdated, and overall organization was so poor that men in battle often lacked supplies. It was this troubled army that in mid-August of 1914 attacked eastward into the German state of East Prussia.

Russia faced one huge geographical problem in the fight against Germany and Austria-Hungary: Poland. Poland was at that time a Russian territory. It was surrounded on the north and west by Germany and on the south by Austria-Hun-

gary. In military terms, it was a salient, or bulge, which would be difficult to defend. To address this problem, Russian military commander General V. A. Sukhomlinov sent the Russian First Army under General Pavel Rennenkampf (1854–1918) and the Russian Second Army under General Aleksandr Samsonov (1859–1914) to invade East Prussia, the easternmost portion of the German Empire. Rennenkampf was to drive due west toward Königsberg; Samsonov was to drive into East Prussia from the south; together, the two armies planned to crush the Germans.

At first the battle went well for the Russians. Rennenkampf crossed into East Prussia with an army that outnumbered the Germans. Though they stalled after their first day of attacks at Stallupönen, the Russians held a strong position and struck a heavy blow against the Germans in the days that followed. The German counterattack had begun badly, with one division commander attacking where he shouldn't have and with German artillery raining shells on its own sol-

General Paul von Hindenburg, Kaiser Wilhelm II, and General Erich Ludendorff.
Reproduced by permission of Corbis Corporation (Bellevue).

diers. Even worse, German general Max von Prittwitz learned that Samsonov's army was moving in from the south. Von Prittwitz panicked and ordered his men to retreat. He believed that East Prussia was lost.

Von Prittwitz's failure in East Prussia alarmed German chief of staff Helmuth Johannes von Moltke (1848–1916). After all, the German war plan depended on holding firm in the east while the war was won in the west. Von Moltke quickly fired von Prittwitz and replaced him with two men who would become key figures in the war: General Paul von Hindenburg (1847–1934) and General Erich Ludendorff (1865–1937). Ludendorff would act as the older Hindenburg's chief of staff. With Hindenburg and Ludendorff in charge, the Germans soon reversed the tide of war in the east and dealt the Russians a mighty defeat at what came to be called the Battle of Tannenberg.

The Battle of Tannenberg

Russian incompetence and German luck soon turned the early Russian triumphs into a disaster of major proportions. After his initial victory, Rennenkampf, who had driven west into East Prussia, misunderstood Germany's actions and didn't press his attack. Instead, he collected his forces for a bigger attack to come. Germany, on the other hand, anticipated Russia's actions perfectly. After all, they had heard the words of the Russians themselves. Lacking codebooks (instructions for sending coded messages), the Russians sent uncoded radio messages back and forth in the open air. The Germans thus learned that Rennenkampf would hold still while Russian general Samsonov, whose troops were driving up from the south, attempted an attack near the town of Tannenberg. Though Samsonov and his troops thought their attack would be a surprise, they soon blundered into the waiting arms of a strong German army.

The core of the Russian army moved north and struck near Tannenberg on August 26 and engaged in heavy fighting against the German forces. Meanwhile, German general von François opened a massive attack on the Russian left flank (side) and began circling around the Russian troops from the southwest; other German forces opened a hole in the Russians'

right flank. By August 29 the bulk of Samsonov's troops were completely surrounded by Germans—and then the killing began in earnest. In his *Short History of World War I* James Stokesbury writes, "The ten-mile-wide trap east of Tannenberg was turned into a vast abattoir [slaughterhouse] of dead and dying horses and men. Soldiers cowered under the shellfire or shot themselves or vainly dashed against the German positions." By the end of the battle the Germans had taken over ninety thousand prisoners, and the Russians had lost another fifty thousand in dead and wounded. Samsonov barely escaped capture. According to Jay Winter and Blaine Baggett, Samsonov wondered aloud to a staff officer, "The Emperor trusted me. How can I face him after such a disaster?" He then wandered into a nearby wood and shot himself to death.

Tannenberg was a great victory for the Germans, and it made the reputation of German generals Hindenburg and Ludendorff, who would later go on to mastermind German war efforts on the Western Front. Encouraged by their victory

German soldiers in action against the Russian army during the Battle of Tannenberg. *Reproduced by permission of Archive Photos, Inc.*

and now aware that the Western Front appeared to be a stalemate, the Germans hoped that they might push forward to finish the defeat of the Russians. But the proud Russians would not give up so easily.

Stung badly by Samsonov's defeat, Rennenkampf's soldiers began to withdraw to defensive positions. The Germans pressed forward, and Rennenkampf's withdrawal turned into a full-scale retreat through the difficult region known as the Masurian Lakes. The region's many lakes and lack of good roadways made travel difficult, and Rennenkampf's tired army struggled to escape. Hoping to protect the bulk of his army, Rennenkampf left two divisions to protect his retreat; though their mission was suicidal, the divisions helped prevent the annihilation of the entire Russian First Army.

Fighting the Austrians

Rennenkampf's army was not the only Russian army engaging in battle. To the south the Russians had massed four armies near an area known as the Pripet Marshes. In Galicia, Austrian general Franz Conrad von Hötzendorf had massed three armies of his own. Late in August these two armies squared off in a strange circling battle. The Russians attacked the weak side of the Austrian army; the Austrian army attacked the weak side of the Russian army. Both armies pushed forward, gaining more territory than they expected, but not in the way that they had anticipated. By the first week in September, the Russians had gained the advantage and began to push deep into Austrian territory. Soon the Russians had gained nearly a hundred miles and were at the foot of the Carpathian Mountains. The Austrians had lost more than 350,000 men and fell back to the city of Kraków.

To the north of Kraków, in Poland, the Germans and Russians squared off again in battles that raged through the fall and into the winter of 1914–15. Hindenburg and Ludendorff did not expect to defeat the Russians in Poland; they merely hoped to wear them out. To their surprise, the Germans advanced nearly to the city of Warsaw before the Russians recovered and drove them back. In early November the Russians attempted an advance of their own, and their Second and Fifth armies pushed westward into the part of Poland known as Silesia. As in Tannenberg, the Germans knew well what was coming, and they nearly succeeded in encircling the Russian armies again. Through an incredible series of marches, the Russians were able to withdraw from the trap sprung by the Germans.

As winter came to the Eastern Front, the Russians settled in to defend their territory. But the Germans were not yet done for the year: They planned a joint attack with the Austrians to begin in January and February. In this effort the Austrians failed to gain any ground with their attacks launched from Galicia, and they actually lost their fortress in Przemyśl and surrendered some 100,000 men. The Germans attacked in the bitter cold of winter in the Winter Battle of Masuria. Though the Russians lost some 200,000 men, the remaining soldiers did not give up.

The Winter Battle of Masuria ended the first stage of war on the Eastern Front. It was a stage in which little went according to plan. The Russian armies had performed poorly and had taken astonishing losses in life and in supplies, and yet they had gained territory to the south and given little ground elsewhere. The Germans had begun with a real scare and then achieved some stunning victories; yet they had little to show for their efforts. And the Austrians had proven themselves incapable of waging war without German assistance. In battles to come, Austrian leaders would step aside as the Germans took over the Austro-Hungarian war effort.

War in Serbia

Given the concentration of fighting in France, Austria, and East Prussia, it was easy to forget that World War I started when a Serbian-backed terrorist assassinated Archduke Franz Ferdinand, the heir to the Austrian throne, in Sarajevo. The Austrians did not forget, however. They wanted to punish the Serbs for their aggression and began attacks on Serbia early in August 1914. The largely Austrian army of three hundred thousand men led by General Oscar Potiorek crossed into Serbia on August 12, 1914, confident that they would quickly defeat the outnumbered Serb forces. But the Serbians had two things in their favor: the terrain and the quality of their soldiers. Austrians crossing into Serbia had to struggle across three wild rivers and were then confronted with the rough, wooded terrain and undeveloped roadways of the Serb interior. Then they had to fight a small but tough Serbian army of two hundred thousand men led by Field Marshal Radomir Putnik. Within two weeks the Serbs had driven the Austrians back across their border.

Potiorek and the Austrian army pushed into Serbia again on September 8, and this time they held onto territory just inside Serbia. The Austrians launched a third offensive in November, and the Serbs—losing men to war and to an outbreak of typhus—gave up their capital of Belgrade and dropped back into the mountains south and east of the city. Then, just when it looked like the Austrians would conquer the small nation, the Serbs drove the Austrians back down out of the mountains and out of Belgrade. According to James Stokesbury, the Austrians had lost nearly half of the 450,000 men they eventually put into the fight against Serbia and the Serbs lost just under half of the 400,000 men they tapped to fight in the conflict. As the winter snows set in, nothing was decided.

Making Serbia Pay

German military commanders took control of Austro-Hungarian war plans in 1915, and they set their sights on defeating Serbia. Part of their plan was to draw Bulgaria, which lay to the east of Serbia, into the war. Germany promised Bulgaria land that Bulgaria wanted in exchange for assistance with the Central Powers war effort, and on September 6, 1915, Bulgarian king Ferdinand I joined the Central Powers alliance and promised to join in a major attack against the Serbs. On October 5 the Central Powers began to attack Serbia on several fronts. From the north, the Austrians launched a massive artillery barrage and then marched on the capital of Belgrade. From the east, Bulgarians swept into the country and cut off major rail lines to the Serb-friendly port of Salonika, Greece (now known as Thessalonoki). Then, the Austrians entered Montenegro, to Serbia's west. The Central Powers had virtually surrounded the northern half of Serbia.

Through October and November the Central Powers drove the poorly armed and poorly supplied Serbians south and west out of their country. French troops tried to come to Serbia's aid, but they were little help. As the cold, wintry weather of November arrived, Serbian troops were forced to retreat out of their country and into neighboring Albania. Serbia had been lost, but German commanders would not allow their armies to push into Albania and Greece (on Serbia's southern border) to gain access to the port of Salonika because they feared that they could not keep the troops supplied. The French reinforced the area, and both sides settled in and prepared to fight again another day. That day would not come until near the end of the war.

Russia in Retreat

Though Russia was able to bring more soldiers into battle than any other army, it had little else going for it. Its economy had been troubled in peacetime, and the demands of war were stretching it to the breaking point. Soldiers couldn't get enough guns or ammunition; civilians couldn't get enough bread or fuel. Soldiers complained that they were sent into war at an unfair disadvantage; civilians in some parts of the country began to speak of revolution. To make matters worse, the ruling family of Czar Nicholas was racked with problems as the czar's powerful wife fell under the influence of a mystic named Rasputin (see sidebar on pp. 98–99). In the midst of this crisis, the Germans decided it was time to deal Russia a final blow.

German chief of staff Erich von Falkenhayn had masterminded the defeat of Serbia and wanted to expand the Central Powers victories in the east by driving the Russians out of Austria. If all went well, his soldiers could drive Russia out of Poland as well. The first major attack in this offensive began from Gorlice, just inside the Austro-Hungarian border, in May of 1915. Writes James Stokesbury in his *Short History of World War I:* "The attack opened on May 2, with a tremendous artillery barrage of an intensity previously unknown on the Eastern Front. The Russians were absolutely pulverized, troops driven crazy by the shellfire, units panicking, whole mobs of men wiped out or rushing to the rear. Within two days the Russian 3rd Army was completely annihilated, [German general August von] Mackensen had taken more than 100,000 prisoners, and his soldiers were into the open country and rolling to the northeast." One Russian commander, quoted in Martin Gilbert's *The First World War,* reported that his army

had been "bled to death." Within a few weeks the Russians were driven north and west out of Austro-Hungarian territory.

Facing a weakened and retreating enemy, Mackensen was ready to push on. In July he turned his forces north and began pushing up the Vistula River and then turned east toward the Russian city of Brest-Litovsk. At the same time, German forces began pushing south out of East Prussia, heading for Warsaw. Russian commander Grand Duke Nicholas, a cousin of the czar, wisely saw that the Germans were preparing to surround the Russian forces, and wanting to avoid another disaster like Tannenberg, he ordered a massive Russian retreat from the Polish salient. By the middle of August, the Germans had pressured Russia back hundreds of miles, and they saw no need to stop. They continued to drive on, pushing the Russians back another hundred miles.

For the Russians, 1915 had been a disaster. They had lost the Russian territory of Poland, and it had cost them nearly two million men, almost half as prisoners. Czar Nicholas

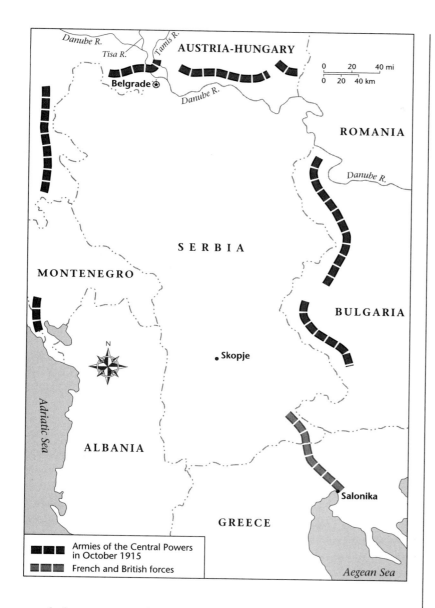

The defeat of Serbia during World War I, 1915.
Reproduced by permission of The Gale Group.

Map legend:
- Armies of the Central Powers in October 1915
- French and British forces

needed a scapegoat for this great disaster, and he found one in his cousin, Grand Duke Nicholas. The czar sacked his cousin and put himself in supreme command of the Russian military. This was perhaps the greatest disaster of all. Not only did Czar Nicholas lack the military experience that was needed for this position, but he also left domestic affairs nearly entirely in the hands of his wife, Alexandra, and her conniving advisor, Rasputin. The only refuge that Russia could take at the end of

The Brusilov offensive and area around the German offensives along the Eastern Front, 1915. *Reproduced by permission of The Gale Group.*

1915 was that the sheer length of its defensive front made any attack difficult. It was not much to cling to.

Russia's Last Gasp: The Brusilov Offensive

With the czar in command of the military and after a winter spent rebuilding the Russian armed forces, the Russians had high hopes for a better year in 1916. Though they did not fare well in a series of battles in the north, they had a new commander in the south who promised to bring a change to Russia's fortunes. General Aleksey Brusilov (1853–1926) had studied the disappointing Russian performances in previous battles and proposed a solution: He would attack quickly over a wide front and thus keep the Austrians and Germans from bringing in their reserves. The Brusilov Offensive, as this attack was called, began on June 4 south of the Pripet Marshes. Following a very short artillery attack, the Russian Eighth Army stormed forward. The Austrians were taken entirely by surprise, and they surrendered in great numbers. Other Russian armies staged similar quick strikes all along the front to the south. The results were impressive—Russian soldiers gained forty miles in some spots, sixty miles in others. The Russians took 400,000 Austrian prisoners and killed or wounded another 200,000; they inflicted nearly 350,000 casualties on the Germans as well.

Over a stretch of front nearly two hundred miles long, Brusilov's armies reclaimed much of the land Russia had lost the previous year. Brusilov would have loved to go further, to once again advance beyond the Carpathian Mountains, but he could not. Losses in battle had weakened Brusilov's Southwest Army Group (as his four armies were called), and supplies were running low. Perhaps more importantly, the German army was bringing reinforcements into place to stop the Russian

Romania's Short War

Romania—which was roughly bounded by the Russian Empire on the north, the Austro-Hungarian Empire on the west, Bulgaria to the south, and the Black Sea to the east—had spent the early years of the war avoiding any involvement. Their king, Carol I, was German born, but most of the government and the people supported the Russians. The Allies eventually earned Romania's support by promising that the Romanians would receive large chunks of Austro-Hungarian Transylvania as their reward for attacking Bulgaria. The Romanians signed on with the Allies in the early fall of 1916, confident that they could join in the advances of the Brusilov Offensive. They were sadly mistaken.

No sooner had Romania joined the Allied war effort than the Brusilov Offensive stalled and the Germans and Austrians began to advance. Romania ignored Allied requests to attack Bulgaria and marched west on Austria-Hungary instead. They met strong German and Austrian armies led by Von Falkenhayn, were stopped dead, and then began to collapse back in retreat. Then the Bulgarian army attacked from the south. Together the Germans, Austrians, and Bulgarians ransacked the country, taking between 300,000 and 400,000 Romanian casualties and capturing Romanian oil fields and the capital. By January of 1917 Romania was no longer capable of waging war.

advance. By October the front stabilized in a line running from the Pripet Marshes south to Stanislau and the Carpathian Mountains. Events on the domestic front in Russia would make this the last of the great Russian military efforts.

Russia's Long Decline

When Czar Nicholas took control of the military at the beginning of 1916, he set in motion a series of events that eventually led to revolution in Russia, and thus to Russia's withdrawal from the war. For thirty years Russia had been torn by the difficulty of industrialization and rapid population growth. Huge rural populations hated their near slavery to local landowners, and masses of urban workers chafed under miserable working conditions. While the masses lived in

The "Evil Monk" Rasputin

The utter collapse of Russian leadership during World War I had many causes; not least among these causes was the influence of a man known as the "evil monk," Grigory Rasputin. Rasputin, as he was most often called, was born a peasant in 1871 (some sources say 1869 or 1872) in the Russian province of Siberia. During his youth Rasputin became known for his drunkenness and his sexual appetite. In his twenties he joined a religious sect that preached that only sin could drive away sin; a fabulous sinner himself, Rasputin became a monk and traveled Russia sinning and preaching.

This strange holy man gained a reputation among some of the nobles in Russia; he was skilled at spinning stories and plotting to gain the attention of the powerful. Rasputin was soon recommended to the most powerful people in all of Russia: Czar Nicholas II and his wife, Alexandra. Rasputin promised to solve the czar and czarina's biggest problem, the hemophilia, or "bleeding disease," of their son, Alexis, the heir to the throne. (The blood of a hemophiliac does not clot properly, and thus the smallest of cuts could potentially cause the person to bleed to death.) For reasons that cannot be explained by science, Rasputin seemed to be able to stop Alexis's bleeding. For this reason he became a close confidant of the ruling family.

poverty, a wealthy class of nobles enjoyed great luxury and privilege. At the top of this class were the czar and his wife, who kept themselves at a distance from society and solved most social problems with force.

In taking command of the military, Czar Nicholas left his wife, Alexandra, in charge of the civil government. Under her guidance, conditions within Russia only grew worse. Alexandra's primary advisor was the mysterious Rasputin, a holy man and mystic who most historians believe was a fraud. Taking Rasputin's advice, Alexandra ordered ever more brutal crackdowns on civil protest. Aristocrats within the government, fearful that Russia could not go on much longer, planned the assassination of Rasputin late in 1916, but even his death was not enough to forestall the disintegration of the empire. As 1917 dawned, Russia was in trouble.

Rasputin's influence on the czar and czarina soon extended beyond his supposed medical powers. A notorious plotter, Rasputin influenced political decisions and conspired to fill government positions with his supporters. People within the ruling class of Russia, including the czar's family, grew to hate Rasputin and the influence he had on the czar. When the czar took over command of the Russian military in 1915, he left the government in the hands of his wife. With Alexandra making all political decisions, Rasputin's power only increased. He fired people he did not like, and he increased his drunken, lecherous ways.

Leading nobles within Russia decided that their troubled country would be better off without Rasputin. Early in 1916, they invited Rasputin to a party and fed him poison—but the poison was not strong enough to kill the durable monk. Determined to be rid of Rasputin, the nobles shot him, beat him, and shot him again. Still he would not die. Finally they wrapped his half-dead body in a carpet and dumped him into an icy river. The coroner's report revealed that Rasputin finally died from drowning. Rasputin was dead, but even though the nobles had succeeded in killing him, they could not halt the collapse of the Russian royal family.

Revolution in Russia

Conditions only worsened in Russia in 1917. Food grew scarce, and prices climbed dramatically. Many Russians faced starvation. Workers staged massive protests and strikes in the major cities of Petrograd and Moscow. The government ordered its loyal mounted troops, the Cossacks, to break up the protests, but neither the Cossacks nor members of the army were willing to repress the people any longer. In fact, many men from the army "switched sides," joining with the people in their protest against the government. The soldiers had demands of their own: They wanted food and an end to the war. By mid-March of 1917 the people of Russia were in all-out revolt against the government.

Convinced by his generals that there was nothing he could do to stop the revolution, Czar Nicholas abdicated (gave up the throne) on March 15. His replacement, his brother

Czar Nicholas II and his family. His wife Alexandra is standing center; daughters Marie, Olga, Tatiana, Anastasia and son Alexei surround him. *Reproduced by permission of Archive Photos, Inc.*

Grand Duke Michael, quickly appointed a provisional (temporary) government. The provisional government tried to bring peace and reform to the country, but it was unwilling to do the one thing that might save it: end the war. And so the revolt continued. Peasants took over land for themselves, and soldiers by the thousands deserted the army. The peasants, workers, and soldiers were all encouraged in their actions by a group of radicals known as "soviets," which literally stood for representatives of the workers. The most radical of the "soviets" were known as Bolsheviks, and they took the revolution to the next stage in the fall of 1917.

The Russian provisional government sealed its fate in the summer of 1917 with an ill-advised military offensive. The Russians attacked again in Galicia and after some small gains were driven decisively back. The Russian offensive had two results: It furthered the disintegration of the military, and it spurred the Bolsheviks to action. In the north, German forces overran the Russian province of Latvia and controlled access to the Baltic Sea. In the cities of Petrograd and Moscow in early November of 1917, Bolshevik leaders Vladimir Ilich Lenin and Leon Trotsky masterminded a swift action that put control of the government in their hands. The Russian Revolution was over, and the Bolsheviks—who promised to end the war and put control of Russian land and industry into the hands of the people—had won.

One of the first actions of the new Russian government was to ask Germany for an armistice, a truce ending the war. Negotiator Trotsky asked that his country, Russia, pay no price for its defeat, but the Germans set a high price on the deal: They wanted independence for many of the states and provinces within the Russian Empire, including Finland, Poland, the Baltic States, and several others. The Germans' request would have ended Russian control over Eastern Europe. The Bolsheviks refused but soon found themselves backed into a corner. The Germans told them they could either give in to German demands or keep on fighting. When the Germans launched further military attacks all along the Russian frontier, the Russians finally gave in. Granting independence to many Russian states and turning over massive amounts of war supplies, Trotsky signed the treaty ending Russia's involvement in the war on March 3, 1918.

Winding Down the War in the East

Russia was not the only country tiring of war in 1917. Austria-Hungary, too, was reeling from the difficulties of waging war. Austria-Hungary's problems were compounded by the death of Emperor Franz Josef on November 21, 1916. The aging emperor had been able to hold together the diverse mix of peoples that made up his empire, and he had stood up to the strength of the Germans. His successor, Charles I, was not able to do either. Charles largely handed over control of the weakened Austro-Hungarian military to the Germans, and he could do nothing to quell demands for an end to the war, which were coming from various ethnic groups within his empire. Charles feared that the empire his great-uncle had built was about to collapse.

The southern end of the Eastern Front, in Bulgaria, had been quiet for some time. A small force of Allied troops moni-

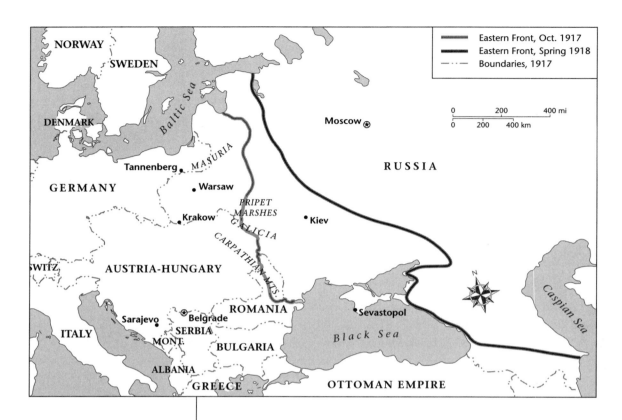

The Eastern Front in October 1917 and spring 1918. *Reproduced by permission of The Gale Group.*

tored events from the Greek city of Salonika, but until 1917 the Allies had been unable to persuade Greece to join their side and wage war on the Central Powers in Bulgaria. By mid-1917 the Greek king, Constantine, was pushed aside; a new government took power and declared war on the Central Powers. Declaring war was one thing, but waging it was another. The Greeks were not willing to pour soldiers into a war against German-backed forces in Bulgaria, so they waited for the Allies, especially the French, to send troops to the region.

By late summer of 1918, a mixed force of some 700,000 men led by French general Franchet d'Esperey began an attack on Bulgaria. Beginning on September 14, the Allies attacked along what was known as the Salonika Front. For several weeks they drove back the mixed Bulgarian and German forces. Bulgarian commanders asked their German bosses to surrender but were told to fight on; in some cases, whole Bulgarian regiments mutinied or surrendered anyway. By late September the Allies—including Greek, French, Serb, British, and Moroccan troops—occupied Bulgaria and Macedonia and were prepared to march into Serbia. On September 28 the Bulgarian government signed an armistice agreement, ending Bulgaria's part in the war. Bulgaria was the first of the Central Powers to surrender, and others were soon to follow.

German military advisors fleeing Bulgaria told the German leadership that their army could not continue in the east. Germany had sent most of its soldiers west to fight against the growing Allied onslaught on the Western Front, and now all of southern Europe seemed ready to collapse. Another German ally, Turkey, surrendered to the Allies on September 30, giving the Allies more strength in the area. Austria-Hungary seemed ready to fragment into a dozen pieces.

Austro-Hungarian Collapse and the End of the War in the East

Austria-Hungary controlled many provinces that had long desired to be independent. Those desires only grew with the war. Poles within Austria-Hungary wanted to combine lands once held by Germany, Russia, and Austria-Hungary into a new country called Poland. Czechs, too, wanted a country of their own. The various Slavic groups—Bosnians, Herzegovinians, Serbians—hoped to join in a Yugoslav nation. With its army collapsing in Italy and its diplomats frantically trying to make peace with the Allies, Austria-Hungary fell apart in the fall of 1918. The Czechoslovaks declared independence on October 21; the Yugoslavs followed suit on October 29. In the days that followed, Austria and Hungary actually seceded from the empire that had borne their names. According to James Stokesbury, "When the imperial government managed at last to sign an armistice with the Allies on November 3, it signed for an empire which in fact no longer existed."

The collapse of Austria-Hungary, along with the surrender of the rest of the Central Powers, posed an enormous problem for the lone remaining Central Powers combatant, Germany. Not only was Germany being hammered by the American-backed Allied powers in the west, but now it stood alone against the world. On November 11, realizing that the war could not go on, a new German government surrendered to the

Allies and ended World War I. The peace negotiations still to come would radically reshape the map of eastern Europe.

For More Information

Bosco, Peter. *World War I*. New York: Facts on File, 1991.

Clare, John D., ed. *First World War*. San Diego, CA: Harcourt Brace, 1995.

"The Great War and the Shaping of the 20th Century." [Online] http://www.pbs.org/greatwar. (accessed October 2000.)

Kent, Zachary. *World War I: "The War to End Wars."* Hillside, NJ: Enslow, 1994.

Macdonald, Lyn. *1914–1918: Voices and Images of the Great War*. New York: Penguin Books, 1991.

Sommerville, Donald. *World War I: History of Warfare*. Austin, TX: Raintree Steck-Vaughn, 1999.

Stewart, Gail. *World War One*. San Diego, CA: Lucent, 1991.

"World War I: Trenches on the Web." [Online] http://www.worldwar1.com. (accessed October 2000.)

Sources

Gilbert, Martin. *The First World War: A Complete History*. New York: Henry Holt, 1994.

Heyman, Neil M. *World War I*. Westport, CT: Greenwood Press, 1997.

Keegan, John. *The First World War*. New York: Alfred A. Knopf, 1999.

Stokesbury, James L. *A Short History of World War I*. New York: William Morrow, 1981.

Winter, J. M. *The Experience of World War I*. New York: Oxford University Press, 1989.

Winter, Jay, and Blain Baggett. *The Great War and the Shaping of the 20th Century*. New York: Penguin Studio, 1996.

The Far-Flung War: Fighting on Distant Fronts

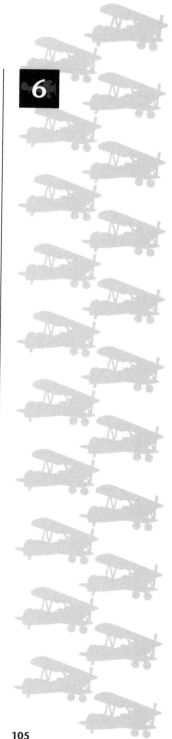

6

World War I began as a European war. The spark that started the war came from Eastern Europe. The major combatants—the Central Powers (led by Germany and Austria-Hungary) and the Allies (led by France, Russia, and Great Britain)—entered the war to protect their territory and their interests in Europe. And the majority of the fighting and the deaths came on two European fronts. But soon after the war started, fighting spread to far-flung European colonies in the Pacific Ocean and in Africa, to the Italian border with Austria-Hungary, and to key strategic points in the Middle East and in western Asia, in what was then known as the Ottoman Empire and is now known as Turkey. Though much of the distant fighting had little bearing on the war, the fighting in Turkey and Italy was especially intense and destructive. As with every aspect of this wide-spread war, it was also very disruptive. This chapter surveys the various distant theaters of operations (areas where combat took place) that turned a European conflict into the first war to be fought all over the world.

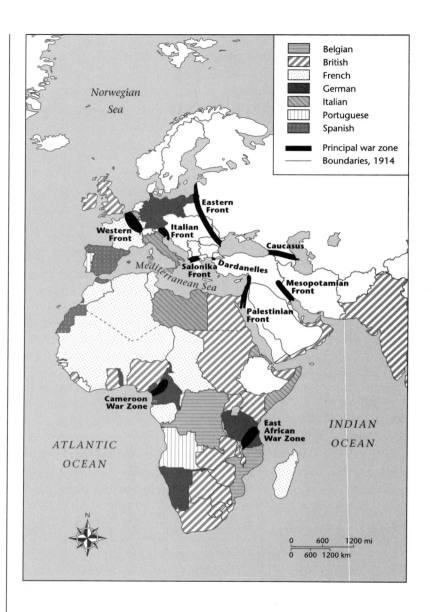

Fighting for the Colonies: The Pacific

In the years before the war started, Germany had worked hard to establish colonies in distant parts of the world. These colonies provided ports for German shipping and supplied raw materials for German industry. Among the most distant of these colonies were several groups of islands in the south and central Pacific Ocean known as the Marianas, the

Carolines, the Solomon Islands, and the Marshall Islands. Germany also controlled a small region on the coast of China called Kiaochow.

Soon after the war began in August 1914, Japan, Australia, and New Zealand raced to strip Germany of these colonies. Japan declared war on Germany on August 23 purely as an excuse to grab German territory in the Far East. By October, Japanese forces had overwhelmed the very small number of German soldiers stationed in the area and had claimed the Marianas, the Marshall Islands, and the Carolines. The Japanese faced a more difficult challenge in Kiaochow. For two weeks, three thousand German marines defended the port city of Tsingtao against a combined Japanese and British force of nearly twenty-five thousand. Surprised at this resistance, the Japanese and British were forced to use artillery and airplane bombing to attack the Germans, who finally gave in and surrendered on November 7.

Australia and New Zealand, countries that were not eager to see Japan's strength in the Pacific grow unchecked, also scrambled to seize Germany's lightly protected lands. New Zealand quickly captured Samoa, and the Germans just as quickly surrendered German New Guinea, the Solomon Islands, and the Bismarck Archipelago to the Australians in mid-September. By the fall of 1914, when the war on the Western Front had just begun, the war in the Pacific ended with Germany badly beaten.

Fighting for the Colonies: Africa

Great Britain and France had long been the dominant colonial powers in Africa, but Germany also claimed four colonies on the continent: Togo, Cameroon, German Southwest Africa (now Namibia), and German East Africa (now Tanzania). When the war began, there was some discussion about not waging war in Africa at all. None of the combatants (except Great Britain) had major military forces on the continent, but the small forces they did have joined the war in late August. A combined force of French and British soldiers overwhelmed a small German force and took Togo on August 26, 1914. The colony, which lay between British and French territories, was quickly divided among the conquering powers.

German Southwest Africa was a huge colony, several times the size of Great Britain. The area is mostly desert and while was lightly populated, it contained rich diamond mines. The Germans wanted to keep it. The British had nearly sixty thousand troops stationed in the neighboring Union of South Africa, many more than the Germans had available. Before the British could attack, however, they had to suppress a rebellion among South Africans who wanted the British out of their country. With this difficulty removed by the end of 1914 the British quickly captured the coast and began the difficult process of rooting the Germans out of the interior. British and South African troops crossed the difficult desert and, with native peoples rising up against the hated Germans, defeated the Germans at Windhoek and Otavi and forced their surrender on July 9, 1915. Though the Germans were defeated, many German settlers remained in the area.

Cameroon also fell quickly, though not without a fight. As in Togo, the Germans had few soldiers in the colony, and these soldiers were aided by poorly trained and only slightly loyal natives. But the Germans did have weather and terrain on their side. The British attacked into Cameroon from Nigeria in the midst of the rainy season (late in August), and they were soon bogged down in the mud. Worse, they had to cross hundreds of miles of nearly roadless territory even to find the German troops. Still, with the British attacking from the north and the French from the south, the Allies quickly gained control of the coast. Rains once again stalled Allied efforts to take the colony, and it wasn't until February 1916 that the French and British drove the Germans out of the area and divided it among themselves.

The most difficult of the fighting in Africa took place in German East Africa. Another huge country—nearly the size of France—German East Africa was rich in resources and had a population of eight million. Allied efforts in German East Africa were flawed from the beginning. Indian troops were assigned to capture key ports, but they landed in the wrong spot, failed to take a town that the Germans had surrendered, and fired on their own troops. By the end of 1915 the Allies still had not entered the colony. Throughout 1915 small military attacks proved fruitless and when the British finally entered the country in force in 1916 their efforts were repeatedly foiled by German forces led by

General Paul von Lettow-Vorbeck. This wily German commander, who led a small force of thirty-five hundred white and twelve thousand native troops, made the best of his limited resources: He staged small raids on the larger British and South African armies who entered German East Africa, and he destroyed bridges and roads to make their progress more difficult. The Allies, with their dramatically bigger armies, chased Lettow-Vorbeck and his forces all over the huge country for the better part of two years and had not yet defeated him when the German surrender on the Western Front in November 1918 made continued fighting unnecessary.

War in the Ottoman Empire

Perhaps the most crucial battles fought outside of Europe were fought in the area occupied by the dying Ottoman Empire (also known as the Turkish Empire or simply as Turkey). The Ottoman Empire—which in addition to Turkey once contained present-day Syria, Egypt, Iraq, the Balkan States, and Palestine, as well as parts of Russia, Hungary, and Arabia —had been in decline since the sixteenth century; by the coming of World War I it was nearly ready to collapse. By 1914, the empire consisted of present-day Turkey as well as narrow strips of land stretching along the coast of the Mediterranean Sea, south along the Red Sea, and southeast along the Tigris and Euphrates Rivers to the Persian Gulf. It was strategically important territory, not only because it physically separated Russia from access to the Mediterranean but also because it contained some of the world's richest oil reserves and key port cities such as Basra (in present-day Iraq). Both the Allies and the Central Powers saw control of Turkey as one key to winning the war.

Turkey had not officially allied with any of the major combatant countries in the years leading up to the war. But

Paul von Lettow-Vorbeck.
Reproduced courtesy of the Library of Congress.

Soldiers on the Romanian Front in the Carpathian Mountains. *Reproduced by permission of Corbis Corporation (Bellevue).*

when Turkish leader Enver Paśa rose to power in 1913, he had friendly dealings with the Germans—which included inviting German military officials to help reform the Turkish army. This meant that Turkey sided with the Central Powers as soon as the war began. Under Enver Paśa's leadership, Turkey conducted campaigns in three distinct areas: along the border with Russia, in the Caucasus Mountains; near the Persian Gulf; and around Egypt and Palestine. Most importantly, it conducted a crucial defensive campaign against concerted Allied attacks in the Dardanelles, a waterway connecting the Mediterranean to the Black Sea.

Fighting in the Caucasus

The biggest of the Turkish army's early attacks came in the Caucasus Mountains, which lay on the border between Turkey and Russia. Fighting in these high mountains would

have been difficult in the summer, but Enver Paśa called for the fighting to begin with the coming of winter. It was a disaster. Fighting in the bitter cold, both sides suffered high casualties. According to *First World War* author John Keegan, one Turkish division lost 4,000 of 8,000 men to frostbite in just four days of fighting. Only 18,000 of the 95,000 Turks who began the battle survived; 30,000 were said to have died of cold, for wounded soldiers simply could not survive in temperatures that dropped to fifty-five degrees below freezing.

When spring came to the mountains, Russia had expanded its claims in the region and provided backing for ethnic Armenians who had long hated Turkish rule. One Armenian regiment slaughtered a group of Turks inside Turkish territory, an action that the Turks would recall when in 1915 they began a systematic and brutal genocide against Turkish Armenians (see sidebar). Turks and Russians continued to fight in the Caucasus through 1915 and 1916. Despite the

Armenian Genocide

On April 24, 1915, several hundred Turkish Armenians were rounded up in the capital city of Constantinople and in other cities throughout the Ottoman Empire. These men—professionals, journalists, and businessmen—were taken from their families and ruthlessly killed by Turkish Muslims. Thus began the killing of hundreds of thousands of Christian Armenians in the first genocide of the twentieth century.

Turks had long disliked the Armenians, most of whom lived in the northeastern corner of the empire, in a region known as Anatolia. The Armenians had a different religion and a different culture than the majority of the people in Turkey, and the so-called Young Turks who came into power in Turkey just before World War I believed that the Armenians could not be trusted and ought to be removed from Turkey. When some Armenian army units fought alongside the Russians against Turkey in the Caucasus Mountains, the Turkish authorities announced that all Armenians should be deported (sent away) from Turkey. It was under the guise of this deportation that the genocide began.

Across Turkey, gangs of thugs began rounding up Armenians, stripping them of their belongings, and sending them on forced marches out of the country. Many of the Armenians died of starvation or exhaustion on their long treks through uninhabited desert. Others were simply rounded up and killed. According to Jay Winter and Blaine Baggett, authors of *The Great War and the Shaping of the 20th Century,* "Between 500,000 and one million Armenians were killed or died of exposure or disease in camps or in the Syrian desert. In the midst of war, a substantial part of a long-established and prosperous civilian community with identifiable religious and cultural characteristics was wiped out."

Though reports of the killings and deportation made their way to the outside world, other countries did nothing to stop the killing. Many governments condemned what was happening, but they claimed they could do nothing until the war was over. By then it was too late for the Armenian people. Among the many people who drew lessons from the Armenian genocide was Adolf Hitler, who would call for the genocide of Jews in eastern Europe during World War II. Trying to justify his actions, Hitler once asked, "Who today remembers the Armenians?" Remembering the Armenians and the Jews killed in the Holocaust is important because it may help prevent any such tragedy from occurring again.

fact that Russia's attention was almost solely focused on battling the Germans and Austrians on the Eastern Front, Russian general Nikolay Yudenich managed to hold Russian ground and fight the war in the Caucasus to a stalemate.

Gallipoli: Allied Hopes Denied

Soon after French, British, and German forces became deadlocked on the Western Front, Allied leaders began looking for a way to change the tide of the war. First Lord of the Admiralty Winston Churchill of Great Britain (who became British prime minister during World War II) proposed that the British use their one area of undisputed strength, their navy, to attack Turkey in the Dardanelles—a small strip of water connecting the Mediterranean to the Black Sea. Control of this waterway would give the Allies a crucial link to Russian ports on the Black Sea. If the Allies could capture the Dardanelles, they could drive Turkey out of the war, link to fellow Allied forces in Russia, and encircle Germany. It was a daring plan.

The Allies began with a combined British and French naval attack on February 19, 1915. They hoped to drive their fleet up the narrow straits, shelling the Turkish forces into submission and landing troops to take Gallipoli, the major city in the region. They were sorely disappointed. Weather forced continual delays, their shells either didn't land in the right places or did too little damage, and Turkish mines laid in the water slowed or blew up Allied ships. Thoroughly frustrated, the Allies prepared for another naval assault on March 18. Newly laid Turkish mines soon ripped this assault to shreds. First the French battleship *Bouvet* blew up and sank, along with seven hundred men, and then three British ships, the *Inflexible,* the *Irresistible,* and the *Ocean,* either sank or were eliminated from battle. The Allies gave up but vowed they would defeat Turkey by other means.

Allied hopes for capturing the Dardanelles soon centered on a coastal invasion along the Gallipoli Peninsula, which lay to the north and west of the Dardanelles. The Allies planned to land on a series of beaches, advance straight uphill to the bluffs overlooking the Mediterranean, and then march inland. They never expected the fierce resistance of a few thousand Turkish soldiers led by a divisional commander named

A 60-pound heavy field gun firing on the top of a cliff at Helles Bay, Gallipoli.
Reproduced by permission of Archive Photos, Inc.

Mustafa Kemal (who would later become Atatürk, the founder of modern Turkey). Undersupplied and outmanned, the Turks dug machine-gun nests and bunkers along the tops of the rocky bluffs and awaited the Allied attack.

Allied troops—including many soldiers from the Australian and New Zealand Army Corps, or Anzacs—landed on the beaches of Gallipoli on April 25. Several divisions landed on deserted beaches and advanced easily uphill in search of an enemy that did not appear. Sadly, they were unprepared for such an event and did not take advantage of it; the Turks soon brought up reinforcements and kept the Allies pinned near the beach. Other divisions faced sheer carnage: Turkish machine gunners sat high above some beaches, holding their fire until British landing craft reached the shore. As these troops crowded to get out of the barges, the Turks opened fire. James Stokesbury, author of *A Short History of World War I,* describes the scene: "Within moments the barges were filled with dead, dying, and wounded, their scuppers running with blood and the water turning a frothy pink around them. Still the soldiers came out of the [landing craft], clambering down the ramps to certain death, and the Turks kept shooting them down until at last they came no more."

By day's end the Allies had landed their troops on shore, but at a far higher cost in lives than they had expected and with far smaller gains in territory. Within a few days the British, the Anzacs, and the Turks were dug in along trenches not far inland. Through May and June the British and Anzac forces tried to drive forward several times, but each time they were repulsed by Turkish defenders who everywhere occupied the high ground. It was the Western Front all over again, and in true Western Front style the British decided that the key to victory was to try again. The final Allied assault on Gallipoli began on August 6. Reinforced with thousands of fresh troops, the Allies smashed into the Turkish defenses, but they measured their gains in feet, not miles. Within three days this assault, like all the others, died. With winter coming on and no sign of change in Gallipoli, the Allies did a sensible thing: They withdrew. By January 9, 1916, the Allies had removed their last man from the Gallipoli Peninsula.

The attack on Gallipoli has gone down in history as one of the bloodiest and most futile of the World War I battles fought outside of Europe. The Allies lost over 265,000 men, while the Turks are estimated to have suffered 300,000 casualties. Turkey's valiant defense kept it in the war until the very end and dashed Allied hopes for a quick way to end the war.

Death in the Desert

Turkey's threat to the Allies in the Middle East can be expressed in one word: oil. The Allies feared that the Turks would gain control of the oil wells discovered in areas surrounding the Persian Gulf. Late in 1914 the British—who had the greatest influence in the area—landed troops at the end of the gulf and took the biggest town in the region, Basra, from the Turks in a short but intense fight. Discovering few Turks in the area, British and Indian forces (India was then a British colony) began to move up the Tigris and Euphrates River valleys toward Baghdad, the major city in Mesopotamia, as this area was called. The British-led forces

British soldiers pulling field guns and caissons across the desert to fight Arab forces in the Persian Gulf.
Reproduced courtesy of the Library of Congress.

soon encountered the toughest enemy in the region: the desert heat. As British and Indian troops drove northward, they stretched their supply lines ever thinner. According to James Stokesbury, author of *A Short History of World War I,* "The temperature was appalling, disease was rife, and the conditions were generally primitive and nasty for everyone." The Allies took the towns of An Nasiriya, on the Euphrates, and Amara, on the Tigris. Cheered by these successes, Allied commanders back in Europe asked for the impossible: They wanted the generals to capture Baghdad.

In the fall of 1916 British forces led by General C. V. F. Townshend began to march up the Tigris River toward Baghdad. They won an important victory when they beat the Turks and captured the town of Kut on September 28; then they prepared to set out across the desert, fortified with the absolute minimum in supplies. By November the British army had come within ten miles of Baghdad, but heavy Turkish defenses and dwindling supplies forced them to turn back. Sensing victory, the Turks trailed Townshend back to Kut, surrounded the city, and held the British under siege.

For four months, and despite repeated attempts by the British to rescue the men at Kut, the Turks held the Allies captive. Finally on April 29 Townshend and his men could hold out no longer. All ten thousand men surrendered to the Turks, making it the single largest surrender in British military history. Four thousand of these men later died while being held prisoner. Though the British held their positions further south, the defeat at Kut was a bitter pill to swallow. But over the course of the war the Turkish forces suffered a general decline. The Allies were able to capture Baghdad from the weakened Turkish army and gained control of Mesopotamia in 1917.

Protecting the Suez Canal

Mesopotamia was essential to the Allies because of its oil supply; the lands between Egypt and Palestine were important for another reason: the Suez Canal. The canal, which connected the Mediterranean with the Red Sea, allowed the Allies to ship goods and troops from India, Australia, New Zealand, and the Far East. When the war started, Britain, which controlled Egypt, closed the canal to the Central Powers. Thus one of the first tasks the Germans wanted Turkey to accomplish was to seize the Suez Canal.

Early in 1915, with the technical advice of German colonel Franz Kress von Kressenstein, the Ottoman Fourth Army under General Ahmed Cemal Paśa planned a daring cross-desert raid on the Suez Canal. Carrying custom-built pontoons, which they would use to span the canal, the army crossed the hostile Sinai desert and attempted to capture the canal. However, they were driven back by the substantial British army in the area.

Alarmed by this early attack, the British kept a strong force in the area throughout the war, and this force eventually set off on attacks of its own. Led by General Archibald Murray, the British captured the Sinai peninsula and built water pipelines and roads to supply their troops as they prepared to advance further up the coast toward Gaza. But with poor planning and failed attempts, the British attacks on Gaza sputtered out. As the British replaced Murray with Western Front veteran

Front line, mid-1917
Italian defensive line, Dec. 1917

The Italian front line during World War I. *Reproduced by permission of The Gale Group.*

General Edmund Allenby, Arab tribes in the region rose up in revolt against the Turks. These Arab tribes wanted to carve countries of their own out of the desert. The stage was set for a British push into Palestine.

Allenby led a daring and aggressive advance on Turkish positions in Palestine during 1917. Attacking first inland against the Turkish flank and then directly at the main Turkish positions along the seacoast, Allenby's force met Turkish troops led by the experienced German general Erich von Falkenhayn. The attack, which started on October 31 and came to an end by mid-December, drove the Turks well backward and led to the Allied occupation of the holy cities of Jerusalem and Bethlehem.

After halting their attacks for nine months, the British began advancing again in September 1918. Allenby scored a decisive victory on September 19 in the Battle of Megiddo, and he chased the Turkish army across the Jordan River and back into the hostile desert. The Brits captured Damascus on October 2 and pushed two hundred miles further to Aleppo within three weeks. They had the Turks on the run, and by mid-October the Turks were ready to talk peace. They signed an armistice agreement on October 30, in which the Turks promised to disband their armies, release all prisoners, and allow the Allies to control their territory. For the once mighty Ottoman Empire, this agreement meant more than mere withdrawal from the war; it signaled the end of the empire's existence. Postwar negotiations stripped the empire of much of its land, leaving only the nation of Turkey. The Ottoman Empire's collapse was also a sign to Germany that the end was near, for now the Allies truly had the Germans surrounded.

Italy

Italy entered the war alongside the Allies for one reason: It hoped to gain land from the Austrians. Prior to the war Italy had been loosely allied with Germany and Austria, but Allied promises of Italian land gains along Italy's border with Austria

lured Prime Minister Antonio Salandra (1853–1931) to side with the Allies. The Italians opened fighting with Austria in May of 1915. The fighting on the Italian Front proved to be a major distraction for the Austrians, requiring men and supplies that the failing Austro-Hungarian Empire did not want to provide. Largely conducted in difficult mountainous areas, the fighting in Italy was never terribly decisive, but it remained an important part of the Allied war effort from 1915 through 1918.

Italian troops and refugees traveling in wagons at the Isonzo Front in northeastern Italy.
Reproduced by permission of Archive Photos, Inc.

Italy's front with Austria was shaped like a large *S* lying on its side. The western curve, bulged downward into the Italian region known as Trentino; the eastern curve stretched upward into Austria. Because so much of this territory was in the mountains, the only place where armies could advance easily was along the coast of the Gulf of Venice, toward the Isonzo River and the Austrian town of Gorizia. Thus, while small forces battled to hold the frontier in Trentino, the Italians sought to defeat the Austrians on the battlefields of the Isonzo. Italy nearly bled to death trying.

The Twelve Battles of the Isonzo

After backing the Austrians up into the mountains east of the Isonzo River, Italian commander Luigi Cadorna ordered his troops to drive over the mountains. Thus began the first of twelve battles of the Isonzo. In four battles through the summer and fall of 1915, the Italian army threw itself against the entrenched Austrian forces. When the winter snows came, the Italians had nothing to show for their efforts. The Isonzo assault opened again in March 1916, with the Fifth Battle; the Sixth through Ninth Battles took the combatants into the fall. The Italians gained only a small amount of land at a massive cost in dead and wounded. The rocky, narrow valleys of the area brought a new kind of injury to the war as artillery shells sent rock fragments in all directions, taking out men's eyes and carving gashes in their flesh.

Though the Italians did not gain much territory in the Tenth and Eleventh Battles of the Isonzo in the summer of 1917, they did succeed in wearing down the Austrian army, forcing the German army to come to the rescue. In the Twelfth Battle of the Isonzo, better known as the Battle of Caporetto, the Germans gained a decisive victory. Launching an aggressive surprise attack on October 24, the Germans and Austrians broke through the Italian lines and started a massive Italian retreat. The Central Powers drove the Italians back nearly seventy-five miles and captured 275,000 prisoners along the way. Many of the Italians simply gave up, for the Italian army's will to fight had been nearly destroyed by their constant, futile attacks. The Italians finally built defensive lines near the Piave River, north of Venice, which they maintained until the end of the war.

Austrian troops advance with flame throwers during the Isonzo campaign.
Reproduced by permission of Archive Photos, Inc.

Little more of significance happened on the Italian front. The Austrians tried to drive the Italians back over the Piave in June 1918, but the Italians held their ground. In October 1918, as Austria collapsed under the pressures of war and a crumbling empire, the Italians mounted a major offensive and drove the Austrians out of Trentino. By then, however, the war was ending, and many Austrian troops simply gave up and let the enemy pass through.

Conclusion

Little had been accomplished in Italy other than the bleeding of the Austrian army. But then little was expected of the battles being fought beyond the Western and Eastern Fronts. The Battle of Gallipoli, which could well have been a turning point in the war if the Allies had accomplished their mission. But the rest of the battles on distant fronts were fought for different stakes than the major operations in Europe were. In some cases, as in the Pacific and Africa, the far-flung battles were fought to steal territory from an enemy who was fighting on the Continent, too busy to defend distant lands. In other cases, as in the battles in Mesopotamia and Palestine, the combatants fought to defend key strategic points or supply lines. Though none of the battles covered in this chapter changed the course of the war, they did help determine the shape of the postwar world, for they sealed the Allied claim to much of the territory previously controlled by the former German Empire and its allies.

For More Information

Gammage, Bill. *The Broken Years*. Cairns, Australia: University of Queensland Press, 1975.

"The Great War and the Shaping of the 20th Century." [Online] http://www.pbs.org/greatwar (accessed October 2000).

Hovannisian, Richard G., ed. *The Armenian Genocide in Perspective*. London: Allen and Unwin, 1985.

"World War I: Trenches on the Web." [Online] http://www.worldwar1.com (accessed October 2000).

Sources

Gilbert, Martin. *First World War Atlas*. New York: Macmillan, 1970.

Keegan, John. *The First World War*. New York: Alfred A. Knopf, 1999.

Stokesbury, James L. *A Short History of World War I*. New York: William Morrow, 1981.

Winter, J. M. *The Experience of World War I*. New York: Oxford University Press, 1989.

Winter, Jay, and Blaine Baggett. *The Great War and the Shaping of the 20th Century*. New York: Penguin Studio, 1996.

The War at Sea | 7

World War I was a land war, with its biggest and most important battles fought on the battlefields of Europe. There were relatively few naval battles in the war, and the important ones were won by the British navy, which succeeded in keeping the German navy pinned down in its ports on the North Sea. This does not mean, however, that affairs of the sea were not crucial to the waging of war. One of the key elements of the Allies' strategy was a naval blockade of Germany; the Allies hoped to starve Germany of the food and raw materials it needed to wage war. Equally key to the Central Powers' war aims was the campaign of submarine warfare that struck at Allied shipping. Although no naval battle decisively influenced the course of the war, the war for control of the seas was vital to the winning of the war.

If one thing seemed certain at the beginning of World War I, it was that Great Britain would rule the seas. With the world's biggest and most powerful navy, Britain seemed likely to continue its long dominance of naval warfare. The German navy was also large and powerful, but German leaders, especially Kaiser Wilhelm, did not want to risk a direct confronta-

British warship HMS
Dreadnought. *Reproduced*
by permission of Archive
Photos, Inc.

tion with the powerful British navy. Therefore, the British were able to trap the bulk of the German navy in its North Sea ports, which lay between the neutral countries of Holland and Denmark. The Germans found their greatest naval successes under the sea, with a fleet of submarines, or U-boats, that did great damage to Allied warships and merchant ships. Had the Allies not figured out how to avoid the German U-boats, as they did by late 1917, the war might have turned out quite differently.

Cruiser Battles

The first naval encounters of the war were small affairs, and they were humiliating if not disastrous for the Allies. These encounters—battles would be too dramatic a word—involved German cruisers (small battleships) scattered around the world. The most troublesome of the German cruisers escaped from the German-held Chinese port city of Tsingtao before that city fell to the Allies early in the war. German admiral Maximilian Graf von Spee (1861–1914) headed east across the Pacific with his cruisers *Scharnhorst* and *Gneisenau;* he sent a lighter cruiser named *Emden* west into the Indian Ocean. These cruisers did their best to terrorize Allied shipping before they were stopped.

The *Scharnhorst* and *Gneisenau* were the most powerful German ships outside the North Sea. With eight 8-inch guns and six 6-inch guns (gun size was measured by the diameter of the shell that could be fired), they were capable of taking on anything smaller than the newest British dreadnoughts, the largest and most heavily armed ships on the sea. Von Spee's squadron shelled French holdings in the South Pacific before moving on toward the southern coast of South America. It was there, on November 1, 1914, that they met up with a small British squadron consisting of older, slower ships manned by crews who had never fired their guns before. With the light fading from the sky and the British ships silhouetted against the setting sun, the two squadrons squared off against each other. Within an hour the more powerful German ships had sunk the British ships *Good Hope* and *Monmouth,* sending nearly fifteen hundred British sailors to their death. This fight, called the Battle of Coronel, was the first British naval defeat in over a hundred years.

Smarting from their defeat, the British sent a squadron of newer, faster ships—including two of their battle cruisers, *Invincible* and *Inflexible*—to the Falkland Islands, which were off the eastern coast of Argentina, in the South Atlantic. Finding and destroying von Spee's German squadron should have been difficult, for the waters in which von Spee could have hidden were huge. But the German admiral helped the British cause by appearing near the Falklands just after the British had arrived. With faster boats and bigger guns, the British made short work of the small German fleet, destroying the *Scharnhorst* and *Gneisenau* and several smaller ships in the Battle of the Falklands on December 8, 1915. In all, eighteen hundred German sailors were killed, and the British navy regained its reputation—at least for the moment.

Emden. Few lone ships did as much damage in World War I as the German light cruiser *Emden.* For two months *Emden* roamed around the Indian Ocean, wreaking havoc on Allied shipping. *Emden* sank some of the ships she encountered; she

captured others and used them for supply or prisoner ships.
On September 22, 1914, *Emden* shelled the Indian city of
Madras, hoping to stir up an Indian revolt against British rule.
In late October she cruised into the Allied port of Penang and
destroyed a Russian cruiser and a French destroyer. Finally, in
the second week of November 1914, the Australian cruiser *Syd-
ney* met and overpowered *Emden,* ending her brief career as the
terror of the Indian Ocean. In all, *Emden* had sunk over 70,000

Cat and Mouse in the Mediterranean

When World War I began, four of the warring nations had ships in the Mediterranean Sea, the body of water between Europe and Africa. Britain and France hoped to control this naval theater, but first they had to rid the sea of Austrian and German ships. With fewer than a dozen ships based at the port of Pola on the Adriatic Sea (a narrow body of water between Italy and Austria-Hungary that opens into the Mediterranean to the south), the Austrians were easily trapped in their port. But the Germans proved more difficult.

A squadron of German ships, including the battle cruiser *Goeben* and the light cruiser *Breslau,* dashed out of port early in August of 1914 and set about disrupting Allied shipping in the Mediterranean. They shelled several Algerian ports and nearly got into a battle with a British squadron. The Allies believed Turkey was neutral and hoped they could trap the German fleet against the Turkish shore and destroy it. But Germany had a trick up its sleeve: Germany and Turkey had signed a treaty joining their forces, and the Allies were unaware of this. The Germans simply sailed through the strait at the Dardanelles (a narrow body of water linking the Mediterranean with the Black Sea) and "sold" their ships to the Turks. The Allies were embarrassed that they had let the Germans get away, and the Turks gained two powerful warships that they used to shell Russian bases in the Black Sea.

tons of Allied shipping (the tonnage of a ship is a measure of the number of tons of water that a ship displaces).

Controlling the North Sea

Three factors kept naval warfare between Germany and Britain from becoming an important element in the war: geography, the size of the opposing navies, and a German reluctance to fight. The German navy was based out of ports on the North Sea, principally the port at Jade Bay. But their routes of access to the open Atlantic, and therefore to the oceans, were thoroughly blocked by the British. To the south, the British navy controlled the English Channel; to the north, the British fleet based at the port of Scapa Flow controlled all access into and out of the north end of the North Sea. Britain's Admiral Fisher described this

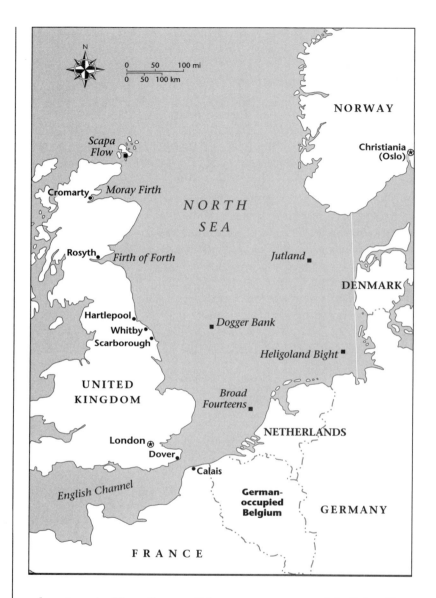

Major North Sea naval battles during World War I, 1914-1918. *Reproduced by permission of The Gale Group.*

advantage to King George V in a passage quoted in John Keegan's *First World War:* "With the great harbour of Scapa Flow in the north and the narrow straits of Dover in the south, there is no doubt, sir, that we are God's chosen people."

There were other circumstances that kept the German navy from becoming an important factor in the war. Most importantly, the Germans were outnumbered: According to Niall Ferguson, author of *The Pity of War,* in 1914 the British

Blockading the Germans

Control of the North Sea was part of the larger Allied strategy of starving Germany of imports, especially imported food. In addition to naval blockades sealing off the North Sea, the Allies established major blockade lines where the Mediterranean meets the Atlantic and in a line stretching north from Scotland to Iceland and on to Greenland. Allied ships stopped all the shipping they could across these blockade lines and seized food and raw materials bound for Germany. The Allies often prevented neutral countries such as Norway, Sweden, Holland, Denmark, and Spain from receiving goods that might be resold to the Germans.

The blockade of Germany was an immediate and enduring success. In 1915 the Allies seized some 3,000 ships headed for German ports; in 1916 they seized 3,388; 2,000 ships were seized in 1917; and in 3,500 ships in 1918. Only 80 ships are known to have evaded interception in this time. Imports to Germany dropped accordingly. Meat imports went from 120,000 tons in 1916 to 45,000 tons in 1917 to 8,000 tons in 1918. Shipments of butter, fish, and live cattle dropped in similarly dramatic ways. These dramatic drops in the quantity of food coming into Germany caused real hardship for the German people. Beginning in 1916, food riots erupted throughout Germany as people clamored for access to limited supplies; many workers were given extra food to get them to perform their jobs. The number of deaths attributed to the blockade rose with each passing year, from 88,235 deaths in 1915, to 121,114 in 1916, to 259,627 in 1917—and finally to 293,760 in 1918. When the German government collapsed and then surrendered to the Allies at the end of 1918, the civilian distress caused by the blockade may have been as important a factor as the military defeats on the Western Front. (All figures are from Martin Gilbert, *First World War Atlas*.)

had twenty-nine large naval vessels to the Germans' seventeen. In tonnage (the measure of the total size of a navy's ships), the British fleet was twice as large as the German fleet. Finally, German naval leaders, from the kaiser down to the various admirals who served under him, did not want to risk losing their newly built navy in open fights with the British. For all these reasons, the Germans never truly challenged the British for control of the seas. They did, however, meet the British in several exciting North Sea battles.

Battle of Heligoland Bight. The first meeting of German and British ships confirmed the kaiser's fears about risking his navy. On August 28, 1914, the British used a decoy force to try to lure the Germans out of Heligoland Bight (a portion of the North Sea between the island of Heligoland and the German coast). The Germans took the bait but tried to spring a surprise of their own by sending out a much heavier force than the British expected. In a disorganized battle fought on misty seas with little visibility, the British succeeded in sinking one destroyer and three cruisers while only taking minor damage. This minor British victory confirmed the Germans' fears and convinced them to lay more mines (floating bombs meant to destroy enemy ships) and post more patrols in the area.

Dogger Bank. The Germans wanted revenge for their defeat at Heligoland Bight, but they labored under a new disadvantage as they prepared for battle in early January of 1915: The British had captured German codebooks and were able to decipher coded messages sent over the radio. Therefore, when the Germans tried to lure a small squadron of the British navy into a trap near Dogger Bank (a submerged sandbank in the central North Sea), the British responded with a large and powerful squadron intent on pounding the Germans. Showing up to spring their trap on January 24, 1915, German ships led by Admiral Franz von Hipper discovered a line of five battle cruisers bearing down on them. The British opened fire while the Germans turned and ran, but what should have been a decisive British victory fell apart when British communications failed and some of their ships sailed off in the wrong direction. In the end the British sank one German armored cruiser, the *Blücher,* while the rest of the German squadron escaped. For the rest of 1915 and into 1916, the Germans stuck to the safety of their ports. But as the stalemate continued on the Western Front, leaders from both Germany and Britain looked to their navies for some way to break the deadlock.

The Battle of Jutland

In May of 1916 British and German naval commanders made the same decision: They would send a powerful force out into the North Sea to scare off any enemy ships in the area. These two decisions, made independently, led to the biggest

battle in naval history. Both sides committed to battle their biggest and best ships—called dreadnoughts—as well as a full range of supporting ships. The British sent forward 28 dreadnoughts, 9 battle cruisers, 11 armored cruisers, 26 light cruisers, 78 destroyers, a seaplane carrier, and a minesweeper. The Germans brought into battle 16 dreadnoughts, 6 pre-dreadnoughts, 5 battle cruisers, 11 light cruisers, and 61 destroyers. The two fleets met in the open sea in an area to the west of Denmark in an area known as Jutland on May 31, 1916.

The Battle of Jutland began when Britain's First Scouting Group (a squadron of battle cruisers), stumbled upon Admiral Reinhard Scheer's main group of German ships. The two navies engaged in a running battle as they moved to the south, directly toward the main force of German dreadnoughts. The British lost two battle cruisers along the way. When the British encountered the main German force, they turned and ran in the opposite direction. The German fleet followed, and the opposing lines of ships continued to shell each

British battleships on the ocean in the Battle of Jutland. *Reproduced by permission of Archive Photos, Inc.*

The Dreadnought

Dreadnought was the name given to the biggest and most powerful ships in the world. These ships were powerful fighting machines, with massive guns and thick armor. They could direct their shelling at targets miles away and could withstand direct fire. They were also equipped with the most modern communication and targeting equipment. By World War I the strength of a modern navy was measured by the number of dreadnoughts it had.

James L. Stokesbury, author of *A Short History of World War I,* described dreadnoughts thusly: "The dreadnought-type battleship was a perfect embodiment of the expertise, the virtues, and the failings of western society. Huge, ponderous yet graceful, those floating cities were massive machines made up of a combination of brute power and the finest instruments the mind of man had yet devised. They could spot a target twenty miles away, and they could hurl at it with pinpoint accuracy a shell that weighed more than a ton. Manned by highly trained and determined technicians, they seemed indestructible. They were dedicated to destruction."

other, this time to Britain's advantage. Still, neither side had brought its dreadnoughts into battle.

The main fleet of the German navy followed the battle north, and thus it ran directly into the main force of British dreadnoughts commanded by Admiral Sir John Jellicoe. The two navies met in a naval situation known as "crossing the T." The British ships were lined up as the top of the T with their guns facing toward the German fleet; the ships in the German fleet were lined up with their bows forward, forming the leg of the T. The most powerful of the British ships opened fire; only the most forward of the German ships could answer. In ten minutes the Germans took twenty-seven hits, while the British took only two. The Germans were forced to turn and run. Admiral Scheer left support ships to cover the German retreat, and they took heavy losses. Fighting continued through the night, but most of the German fleet slipped away under cover of darkness back to their home base. The Germans had escaped a major defeat.

The Battle of Jutland was the most dramatic naval battle of the war, with the biggest ships on earth lobbing shells at each other over great expanses of water. It is also the subject of continuing controversy over who won the battle. The British lost more ships and more men, though more of the surviving German ships were damaged than the British. Most historians now agree that the British won the battle, if only because they kept control of the North Sea. In any case, the two navies never fought again, for the German navy stayed in port and left the fighting at sea to the deadly U-boats.

The Power of the Submarine

With imports virtually halted by the powerful Allied blockade and with the German navy trapped in North Sea ports by the British, Germany seemed to be losing the battle for control of the seas. German naval efforts would have been a complete failure if not for one thing: the success of submarine warfare. Naval officers from every nation had no great expectation for submarine warfare at the beginning of the war, but German successes as early as 1914 convinced the Germans to use submarines—they called them U-boats, for underwater boats—as a major element in their naval strategy.

The Germans scored their first U-boat success in the North Sea, where they had eighteen active subs. On September 5, 1914, submarine *U-21* sank the British cruiser *Pathfinder;* just a few weeks later, *U-9* torpedoed the British cruiser *Aboukir,* then sank the cruisers *Hogue* and *Cressy* when they stopped to rescue the first ship's men. With these strikes the Germans realized the sub's power: It could move undetected and torpedo ships that had no idea the subs were there. Allied ships now traveled with the troubling knowledge that an invisible enemy might sink them at any time.

By 1915 the Germans decided to unleash their new weapon on merchant shipping (ships carrying goods, rather than warships), in direct violation of maritime law. Maritime law (laws governing the behavior of ships at sea) required attacking ships to stop a merchant vessel and allow the crew to escape on lifeboats before the vessel was destroyed. Because submarines worked best when they remained hidden from view, German submarine captains ignored these rules and sank merchant ships at will. When a German sub sank the British liner *Lusitania* in 1915, killing 128 Americans, the United States protested and threatened the break off relations with Germany.

Germany did not want the United States to enter the war. Beginning in May 1916, German naval commanders limited U-boat attacks on unarmed ships, avoiding especially U.S. vessels. But as the war on land grew increasingly desperate, the Germans could no longer afford to hold back one of their most potent weapons. On February 1, 1917, the Germans returned to unrestricted submarine warfare, attacking merchant ships. Their goal was the same as the goal of Britain's naval blockade: They wanted to starve the enemy into giving up the fight.

Captured German submarine UC5 moored at Sheerness. *Reproduced by permission of Archive Photos, Inc.*

Unrestricted Submarine Warfare

The "sink on sight" campaign that the Germans unleashed in 1917 had an immediate impact. By this time the Germans had 148 U-boats in active service, and they began sinking massive numbers of Allied and neutral ships. In 1917 alone, the U-boats sank over a thousand British ships. The damage was greatest early in the year. In February U-boat attacks sent 520,412 tons of cargo to the bottom of the sea; this was followed by 564,497 tons in March and 860,334 tons in April, according to John Keegan in *The First World War*. German military planners estimated that if they could sink 600,000 tons a month, they could starve Britain out of the war. By May the British government estimated that they had only a six-week supply of food left in the entire country. The U-boat strategy was working; if the Allies couldn't figure out how to stop the subs, Britain would soon be out of the war.

Stopping the Underwater Menace

The German sub attacks helped draw the United States into the war in April 1917, just as the Germans had feared, but the Americans initially had little to offer to combat the sub menace. Depth charges (bombs that were dropped into the sea and that exploded when they reached a certain depth) and mines were not the solution, because not enough of them could be laid across shipping channels to stop the submarine menace. Then, thanks to the suggestion of an American admiral, an old idea that British leaders had discarded—the convoy—was tried again. A convoy was a group of ships that sailed together, protected on all sides by armed vessels and sometimes aided by observation balloons that floated above the convoy and allowed spotters to see subs from high in the air. The first convoy was tried on April 28, 1917—and it made it from America to Great Britain without a loss.

Soon, more and more of the merchant ships bringing food and war supplies to Britain traveled in convoys. Losses from U-boat attacks dropped to 511,730 tons by August and 399,110 tons by December. American troops traveled to France in convoys as well and were unmolested by German submarines. The Allies also used other means to combat the subs: They dedicated more airplanes to spotting subs in busy shipping areas and laid hundreds of thousands of mines in shipping channels. But it was the convoy that made the difference, effectively ending Germany's attempt to drive Britain from the war. With Britain still fighting and American troops joining Allied soldiers on the battlefields of Europe, the Allies finally claimed victory in November of 1918.

For More Information

Bosco, Peter. *World War I*. New York: Facts on File, 1991.

Clare, John D., ed. *First World War*. San Diego, CA: Harcourt Brace, 1995.

"The Great War and the Shaping of the 20th Century." [Online] http://www.pbs.org/greatwar (accessed October 2000).

Halpern, Paul G. *A Naval History of World War I*. Naval Institute Press, 1994.

Stewart, Gail. *World War One*. San Diego, CA: Lucent, 1991.

Sources

Ferguson, Niall. *The Pity of War: Explaining World War I*. New York: Basic Books, 1999.

Gilbert, Martin. *First World War Atlas*. New York: Macmillan, 1970.

Heyman, Neil M. *World War I*. Westport, CT: Greenwood Press, 1997.

Keegan, John. *The First World War*. New York: Alfred A. Knopf, 1999.

Milford, Darren. "World War 1 Naval Combat." [Online] http://www.worldwar1.co.uk/ (accessed November 2000).

Sommerville, Donald. *World War I: History of Warfare*. Austin, TX: Raintree Steck-Vaughn, 1999.

Stokesbury, James L. *A Short History of World War I*. New York: William Morrow, 1981.

Technology

8

The First World War caused more death and destruction than all the wars that came before it. The reason for the slaughter was twentieth-century firepower. Powerful new weapons such as the machine gun halted military movements and killed men by the thousands. A British officer, quoted in William G. Dooly Jr.'s *Great Weapons of World War I,* observed the effects of machine-gun fire at the Battle of Mörhange-Sarrebourg in 1914:

> *Whenever the French infantry advance, their whole front is at once regularly covered with shrapnel and the unfortunate men are knocked over like rabbits. They are brave and advance time after time to the charge through appalling fire, but so far it has been to no avail . . . The officers are splendid; they advance about 20 yards ahead of their men as calmly as though on parade, but so far I have not seen one of them get more than 50 yards without being knocked over.*

Machine guns were not the only weapons to radically reshape the nature of modern warfare. Tanks, flamethrowers, airplanes, and submarines—all products of advanced technology—changed the way armies faced each other in battles on land, on the sea, and in the air.

Reproduced courtesy of the Library of Congress.

Machine Guns

"Perhaps no invention has more profoundly modified the art of war than the machine gun," observed U.S. secretary of war Newton D. Baker, according to William G. Dooly Jr. in *Great Weapons of World War I.* Indeed, the machine gun was made for mass murder. Unlike rifles, which could shoot one bullet at a time and were accurate within about a thousand yards, heavy machine guns that were mounted on wheeled carts could fire up to five hundred rounds per minute. Light machine guns weighing between sixteen and twenty-eight pounds could fire magazines of up to forty-seven rounds. Both heavy and light machine guns had an accuracy that far exceeded the rifle's. The French 37mm gun Model 1916 had a range of about a mile and a half, for example.

Military planners did not foresee the importance of the machine gun. War strategists had been trained to rely on large numbers of trained, professional foot soldiers who would

World War I: Almanac

engage in close, hand-to-hand combat to win wars. As the British planned their entrance into World War I, the Ministry of Munitions considered two machine guns per battalion to be "more than sufficient," according to Dooly. The Battle of Loos in 1915 demonstrated how devastating the machine gun was to advancing armies. When a line of British soldiers came within a thousand yards of a defensive line of Germans, the machine gun proved its effectiveness. Dooly quotes a German reserve regiment's observations:

> Ten columns of extended line could clearly be distinguished, each one estimated at more than a thousand men, and offering such a target as had never been seen before, or even thought possible. Never had the machine-gunners such straightforward work to do nor done it so effectively. They traversed to and fro along the enemy's ranks unceasingly. The men stood on the fire-steps, some even on the parapets, and fired triumphantly into the mass of men advancing across the open grassland. As the entire field of fire was covered with the enemy's infantry the effect was devastating and they could be seen falling literally in hundreds.

German machine gun corps protecting the flank of advancing troops.
Reproduced by permission of Archive Photos, Inc.

What Good Was a Hole in the Ground?

Attempting to push further into France in 1914, the Germans were forced into retreat at the Battle of the Marne. But German forces didn't flee far. Their weapons were better for defense; what they needed was a safe place to hide so they could shoot at the Allies. Trenches were that safe place: Ten-foot deep ditches in the ground could protect soldiers and effectively halt the enemy.

The Allies and the Central Powers both dug a variety of trenches. The main battle trenches were dug in zigzag patterns to protect against attack. Supporting trenches were also dug to create protected pathways for communication with headquarters and routes for supplies. Some trenches were open to the air, while others had wooden covers or were actually dug underground. These holes in the ground became parallel lines of trenches stretching 475 miles between the Belgian coast and Switzerland by the end of 1914. Both sides had machine guns positioned in frontline trenches to prevent advances and along second- and third-line trenches to cover any breakthroughs. Each line of trenches was protected by tangles of barbed wire, which were meant to snag any soldiers who had managed to cross the short stretch of land between the opposing trenches, called no-man's-land.

Trenches proved the effectiveness of the defensive weapons on both sides. Trenches halted troop movement. In his *World War One Source Book,* Philip J. Haythornthwaite quotes Canadian general Sir Edwin Alderson's advice to his soldiers in 1915: "Do not expose your heads, and do not look around corners, unless for a purpose . . . the man who does so is stupid . . . If you put your head over the parapet without orders, they will hit that head."

New weapons needed to be invented to break through the heavily defended enemy trenches and to cross no-man's-land, which artillery bombardments had turned into rough, ruined, nearly impassable ground. Soon armies tried poisonous gas and tanks to open holes in trench lines.

Within two years, after the Germans had used the rapid-fire weapons to mow down thousands of charging men and effectively stymie the Allied effort along the Western Front, Britain's Ministry of Munitions increased the allotment of machine guns to thirty-two per battalion. The Allies and the Central Powers both began to group machine guns along lines of trenches to hold off any advancement. By the end of the war, the machine

gun was recognized as one of the most essential weapons for regiments. Between 1912 and 1919, the U.S. Army increased its provisions from 4 machine guns per regiment to 336.

Poisonous Gas

Unable to penetrate the Allied trenches along the Western Front with artillery or with waves of soldiers armed with machine guns, the Germans introduced an insidious new

weapon on April 22, 1915. A German airplane dropped canisters in no-man's-land. Breaking on impact, the canisters released yellowish green fumes that wafted slowly toward the French and African troops near the Belgian town of Ypres. As the fumes reached the Allied forces, soldiers realized the cloud was poisonous chlorine gas. Quoted in Dooly's *Great Weapons of World War I,* one French doctor at Ypres expressed his horror: "I had the impression that I was looking through green

glasses. At the same time, I felt the action of the gas upon my respiratory system; it burned in my throat, caused pains in my chest, and made breathing all but impossible. I spat blood and suffered from dizziness. We all thought we were lost." The gas opened a four-mile gap in the Allied line, but the Germans failed to exploit the gap: Fearful German soldiers advanced slowly behind their terrible new weapon, and nightfall hid the damage the gas had done. By morning, the Allied forces had sealed the gap, and the Germans' attack had accomplished nothing but to display the horror of chlorine gas.

Quickly, both sides developed gas masks. At first, soldiers held chemically treated cotton pads over their noses and mouths. Later they wore fabric face masks soaked in chemicals, and finally soldiers on both sides wore respirators with charcoal filters.

Although the world was outraged by the use of poisonous gas (after the war, its use was banned by international agreements), both Allied and Central Powers forces used vari-

German storm troopers emerging from a thick cloud of phosgene gas laid down by German forces as they attack British trench lines. *Reproduced by permission of Corbis Corporation (Bellevue).*

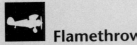

Flamethrower

When soldiers succeeded in crossing no-man's-land and entered enemy trenches, new weapons were needed. Flamethrowers were short-range weapons that squirted pressurized streams of a burning mix of gas and oil; both stationary and portable versions were made. Flamethrowers could literally blow a wall of flame into trenches or passageways in fortifications, burning alive all those inside. After the Germans introduced the weapon in 1914, each country made their own versions of flamethrowers. The French flamethrower, named the Schilt after its inventor, could shoot eight to ten 30-yard bursts of flame or one 100-yard blast.

Flamethrowers were especially good at clearing trenches and forcing the surrender of soldiers in dugouts. The Germans used ninety-six flamethrowers at Verdun in 1916, and it is estimated that there were 653 subsequent flamethrower attacks during the war. The drawback to these weapons was their enormous fuel requirement. In his *World War One Source Book,* Haythornthwaite notes that "one mile of front line (requiring 30 Livens projectors [a type of flamethrower]) would consume about 1,000 gallons of petrol per minute . . . an hour of such operation using more fuel than the entire French army transport service's daily need in 1917–1918." Though effective, the flamethrower would not be fully developed until the Second World War.

ous gases against each other for the remainder of World War I. Armies used several types of gases. Some were lethal, such as the cyanides used by France. Others were irritants. The irritant gas phosgene was used by all countries and caused great suffering to unprotected soldiers, who would get watery eyes, sneezing fits, and blisters on exposed skin; phosgene also scarred the soldiers' lungs. Mustard gas was a persistent irritant that could remain on the battlefield for days.

Casualties from gas attacks totaled nearly 800,000 soldiers during the course of the war. Although the percentage of deaths resulting from gas attacks was relatively low—only 2 percent of American gas casualties died—poisonous gas represented one of the most dreaded and horrifying realities of modern warfare. According to Dooly, "It symbolized the death of individual bravery, initiative, and skill."

Tanks

Even though some forward-thinking engineers proposed prototypes of tanks as early as 1907, it was not until no-
man's-land was thoroughly blood soaked that a joint army-
navy committee formed to build the first tank. The Mark I
prototype, built in Britain in 1915 and affectionately called
"Big Willie," entered the field on September 15, 1916. The
twenty-six-foot-long, twenty-eight-ton tank required a crew of
eight to maneuver it as it lumbered at three miles per hour

British Mark A Whippet
Medium tank advancing
through the mud to
penetrate the German lines
at Morcourt; only two
hundred of these tanks
were ever manufactured.
*Reproduced by permission of
Archive Photos, Inc.*

A New Use for an Obsolete Weapon

World War I was notable for the incredible advances in technology that changed the way wars were fought. But a weapon that had not been used for nearly 250 years became one of the most important weapons for trench warfare. Mortars—short-range artillery weapons designed to lob bombs—had been introduced in 1673 to blow up forts but had rarely been used since the eighteenth century.

At the beginning of the war, the Germans massed about 150 mortars to defend their forts near Metz. But when fighting along the Western Front bogged down into trench warfare later in 1914, the mortars were moved to the front-line trenches to throw bombs into the French trenches a few hundred feet away. The

mortars could destroy the barbed wire barricades protecting the Allied trenches from troop advances. The Germans, with their mortars of various sizes, "were masters with the trench mortar from beginning to end," according to Dooly.

The Allies did not have similar mortars to use in counterattack, so they searched museums for suitable mortars from past wars and used them as models. Until the French introduced their first 58mm trench mortar in 1915, Allied soldiers on the front lobbed makeshift bombs made of nails and explosive powder. The Allies did not develop mortars as mobile as the *Minenwerfer* (German mortars) until near the end of the war, when the French introduced their 150mm mortar in 1918.

across a battlefield. Thirty-two tanks started out across ground that had been mangled by artillery bombardments. The nine tanks that reached their destinations forced the surrender of three hundred Germans and captured the village of Flers.

The first tanks were useful, but they did not prove to be the dominant offensive weapon that their inventor, British lieutenant colonel Ernest D. Swinton, had imagined. Back at the drawing board, tanks went through several more prototypes. The Mark IV won the tank the place it deserved in offensive attacks. On November 20, 1917, four hundred Mark IVs advanced across the torn-up no-man's-land at Cambrai. They smashed through barbed wire, and proceeded to capture six and a half miles of a double line of German trenches within twelve hours, with only four thousand casualties. German

General Paul von Hindenburg lamented that the battle at Cambrai taught the Germans the potential benefits of tanks in modern warfare. That the tanks could smash over barricades and undamaged trenches shocked the Germans.

In 1918 better tanks punched holes in German lines at Soissons and Amiens, forcing the Germans into retreat. The Whippet tank, used in these battles, weighed 15.7 tons and was twenty feet long. A crew of three could speed along in it at 8.3 miles per hour. By war's end, tanks had become a promising part of modern warfare.

Air Warfare

For years, armies remained locked in bitter conflict along static lines of defense that stretched for hundreds of miles. Powerful weapons like the machine gun and poisonous gas rendered individual heroics almost obsolete. But in the air, pilots of newly designed bombers and fighter planes became World War I's glamorous heroes.

When the war began, aviation was not very advanced. Armies used balloons to observe enemy movements on the ground and to protect whole cities with steel curtains up to ten thousand feet high. Germans began dropping bombs from zeppelins just days after their first attack on Liège, Belgium, in 1914 and continued to plague civilians with bombings until a few months before the armistice. England became the prime target of these German zeppelin raids, which reached a peak in 1916 with 126 raids over England.

At the beginning of the war, no country foresaw the usefulness of airplanes. France had 120 planes, Britain had 113, and Germany had more than 200, but not all of these planes were military types. Airplanes were only observation tools at the beginning of the war. They were used to spot artillery, take photographs, and drop messages to ground troops. Most planes could scarcely carry the pilot and enough fuel to complete a flight, but planes were still an important tool: A single plane could survey what once took a whole regiment of cavalry to see.

Pilots quickly realized that airplanes could mount attacks as well. Some pilots packed bricks to throw at other

Anglo-French SPAD VII biplane. With synchronized fire and fast turn of speed, this aircraft helped to restore the Allied position, which was suffering under the might of the German Fokkers. *Reproduced by permission of Archive Photos, Inc.*

pilots or rifles to shoot enemy planes. Paris was the first victim of a bombing raid; a German plane dropped four bombs on August 30, 1914. Realizing the potential offensive capabilities of the airplane, the opposing sides began focusing their energy on improving airplanes' war-worthiness. Guns were the main weapon needed by fighter pilots. Many different plane designs tried to mount guns in places that posed the least risk of shooting the plane's propeller; cockpits for gunners were made on the side of the plane or positioned in front of the propellers.

Aces

On October 5, 1914, French pilot Joseph Frantz and his gunner, Louis Quénault, engaged in the first aerial combat of the war, shooting down a German plane and killing the pilot and his passenger. French pilot Adolphe Pégoud became the war's first ace, shooting down six German planes in 1915. In January of 1915 French pilot Roland Garros invented the first deflector to enable machine guns to shoot between propeller blades. After a plane equipped with one of the deflectors was captured by the Germans in 1915, Garros's invention was perfected by Dutch engineer Anthony Fokker, who was working for the German army. According to Thomas R. Funderburk, Fokker's more sophisticated synchronizer began what the British called the "Fokker Scourge," a German strategy to prey on unarmed or single Allied planes flying reconnaissance missions. The British soon ordered reconnaissance missions to include at least three armed planes.

Nations honored pilots who shot down at least five enemy planes; these pilots were referred to as "aces." French pilot Paul-René Fonck shot down 75; his comrade Georges-Marie Guynemer brought down 53. Eddie Rickenbacker became America's hero, shooting down 22 planes and four balloons. But German pilot Manfred von Richthofen, known as the Red Baron, was the most successful ace of all. Between 1916 and 1918, the Red Baron shot down 80 enemy planes, more than any other pilot on either side.

Parachutes did not become standard issue for military pilots until after World War I, so early combat pilots experimented with flying techniques. The fancy combat maneuvers taught in rigorous flight schools and featured in military air shows in the twenty-first century were made up on the spot by the combat pilots of World War I. Pégoud, wanting to learn as much as he could about flying, was an especially inventive pilot. He tested his plane's capabilities by trying things like flying upside down. Of his experimentation Pégoud said, "If I kill myself, so what? One less aviator. But if I succeed, how many valuable lives may be saved for aviation," as quoted in Funderburk's *Early Birds of War*. Other pilots learned new techniques accidentally. Convinced his death was imminent, one pilot accidentally discovered how to survive when a plane starts spiraling downward. The pilot of the plunging plane decided to speed up his coming death and pushed the plane into full throttle. Instead of speeding him into the ground, his maneuver brought the plane under control and became a valued combat technique he lived to teach others. Pilots soon learned to do spins, half-rolls, and climbing turns, among other things.

A unique witness to the incredible advancements in aviation during World War I was Roland Garros. A skillful pilot

before the war, Garros set an altitude record in 1912, and in 1913 he became the first person to fly across the Mediterranean Sea. He contributed the first crude mechanism for shooting bullets between spinning propeller blades in 1915. Garros spent three years as a German prisoner of war between 1915 and 1918. He escaped and returned to France to find aviation advanced well beyond his dreams. Planes now flew twice as high and twice as fast as Garros had ever seen. Quoted in Funderburk's *Early Birds of War,* Garros noted, "I am a novice now! . . . I used to say that the progress which would be achieved in three years would surpass imagination, but I never thought I would be the first victim of that progress." Garros started over, returning to military flight school. On October 5, 1918— exactly four years after the first aerial combat of Frantz and Quénault— Garros was shot down and killed by the Germans.

Submarines

At the beginning of World War I, huge battleships were deemed the most important naval weapon. The British *Dreadnought,* a battleship with one-foot-thick steel armor, steam turbines to power it two knots (a unit of speed used for ships that is equal to one nautical mile per hour, or 1.15 land miles per hour [1.85 kilometers per hour]) faster than any other warship, and ten 12-inch guns, became the ideal battleship and started an arms race between Britain and Germany. (In fact, the word "dreadnought" soon became the generic name for any huge, heavily-armed battleship.) By 1914 Britain had twenty-four dreadnoughts, and Germany had fourteen. At the start of the war, Britain used its dreadnoughts and other, smaller surface ships to block German ports from receiving supplies.

In 1914 submarines were not seen by either side as essential components to a successful navy. But the Germans quickly identified these "underwater boats" (U-boats) as the best defense against the British blockade. Germany entered the war with twenty-four submarines, massive vessels averaging over five hundred tons' displacement and stretching from 150 to 200 feet long. With four or five torpedo tubes and mounted guns ranging in size from two inches to almost six inches, these submarines were capable of mounting devastating offensive attacks. In 1914 Germany began building submarines at a furious pace, doubling its fleet by the end of the year. By the end of the war, Germany had built nearly four hundred submarines, of which more than half were destroyed.

In 1915, German submarines began attacking ships bringing supplies to Britain. The submarines did considerable damage in 1915, sinking 396 Allied and neutral ships, more than twice the number lost to other ships or mines. But the attacks on merchant shipping outraged neutral countries,

French soldiers waiting in a trench, just before zero hour. *Reproduced courtesy of the Library of Congress.*

especially the United States. In 1915 a German U-boat sank the passenger liner *Lusitania,* which was supposedly carrying munitions to Britain. The death of more than a thousand of the ship's passengers, including 128 Americans, forced the United States to threaten entrance into the war. Hoping to keep America from joining the war, Germany promised to warn ships before attacks so the crew and passengers could evacuate. For a year and a half Germany held back its use of submarines, but by early 1917 military leaders decided that they had little chance of winning the war without using these powerful underwater weapons. In February of 1917 the Germans resumed unrestricted submarine warfare. (For more on submarine warfare see Chapter 7: The War at Sea.)

Germany's return to stealthy U-boat attacks on Allied shipping was an immediate success. The subs sank hundreds and hundreds of ships bringing food and supplies to Great Britain and France. In 1917 German submarines sank 2,439 Allied ships. It looked like the Germans might succeed at their goal of starving the British into submission. Allied navies were desperate to stop submarine attacks. They tried to arm commercial ships and increase submarine patrols, but it was difficult to halt the invisible menace. Finally the Allies began sending large groups of ships across the sea together in convoys. A squadron of armed boats, which surrounded the merchant ships and could fire on any submarine that surfaced to attack them, escorted these convoys. The Allied convoy system was a great success, allowing the safe passage of 88,000 ships, with losses of only 436 ships. The convoy system also destroyed more submarines than ever before, sinking 74 subs in 1918. Convoys didn't stop sinkings altogether, but they limited the damage greatly because the Allies no longer sent lone ships across the open seas. Even if one ship was sunk, many others now made the passage safely. The convoy system largely removed the danger from U-boats and helped the Allies win the war.

Conclusion

Modern technology and industrial capacity combined in World War I to create some of the most powerful weapons ever used in warfare. Tanks, flamethrowers, machine guns, submarines, and airplanes were all tested and proved in battle. There were hints of other technological advances as well. For example, World War I saw the first aircraft landing on a ship at sea and the first torpedo attack on a ship from a fighter plane. All of these technologies would be improved and made more powerful during the Second World War (1939–45). Tanks would become faster, more agile, and more resistant to fire-power, and would help prevent stalemate in the Second World War. Airplanes would fly faster and further and carry more weapons; artillery would become more accurate and more mobile. Unfortunately, these new, modern weapons allowed military planners to wage a second world war that resulted in even more deaths than the first.

For More Information

Gilbert, Martin. *The First World War: A Complete History.* New York: Henry Holt, 1994.

Stokesbury, James L. *A Short History of World War I.* New York: William Morrow, 1981.

"The Weapons of World War One." [Online] http://www.iol.net.au/~conway/ww1/weapons.html. (accessed May 2001.)

"Weapons of World War I." Discoveryschool.com. [Online]. http://school.discovery.com/homeworkhelp/worldbook/atozpictures/lr001160.html. (accessed May 2001.)

Sources

Clare, John D., editor. *First World War*. San Diego: Harcourt Brace, 1995.

Colby, C. B. *A Colby Book about Aircraft of World War I: Fighters, Bombers, Observation Planes*. New York: Coward, McCann and Geoghegan, 1962.

Dooly, William G. Jr. *Great Weapons of World War I*. New York: Bonanza Books, 1969.

Funderburk, Thomas R. *The Early Birds of War*. New York: Grosset and Dunlap, 1968.

Haythornthwaite, Philip J. *The World War One Source Book*. London: Arms and Armour Press, 1992.

The Home Front: Fighting a Total War

9

Life for the soldiers fighting on the Western Front in World War I was a terrible ordeal. Pinned down in muddy trenches for days on end, bombarded with exploding shells from a nearby enemy, and subject to violent and painful death at any moment, soldiers were plunged into what seemed like an endless struggle for survival. Civilians rarely faced the possibility of violent death, but these people back home did suffer severe disruptions in their lives as a result of war. During World War I, while soldiers fought on battlefronts, all civilians were said to be fighting on a front of their own—the "home front."

The idea of a home front was created by the complete mobilization of both soldiers and civilians in the major combatant nations that fought in World War I. In previous conflicts, armies met on battlefields that were removed from civilian population centers and noncombatants were rarely touched by the war unless a member of their family was killed. Wars were short and armies were comparatively small and manned by professional soldiers. World War I changed all this. Armies fought in and around population centers, disrupting daily life in battle areas. Huge numbers of men were conscripted into (forced to join) the armies. The governments of Great Britain, France, and Germany reordered their economies to serve the war effort. Civilians were asked to perform new jobs and give up many of their conveniences in order to help the war effort; every member of society was mobilized in the single goal of defeating the enemy. In short, World War I brought "total war" to Great Britain, France, and Germany. This chapter assesses the effects of total war on the home front.

Creating a Wartime Economy

When the German army marched across the Belgian border on August 4, 1914, it triggered the military mobilization plans of both Germany and France. Trains, trucks, horse-drawn wagons, and soldiers all moved into place in accord with war plans that had been developed years earlier. But the movement of soldiers to the growing battlefronts of World War I represented only one portion of the mobilization efforts of the major combatant nations. All across Germany and France a chain of actions began that brought not only the soldiers but nearly every person in each nation into the war effort. Soon Great Britain would be involved in a similar effort.

Because Germany was already heavily industrialized and the government enjoyed a very direct control over civil life, Germany was the quickest to make the transition to a wartime economy. The German government established a War Raw Materials Division of the Ministry of War, under the charge of prominent businessman Walther Rathenau. Rathenau quickly organized and coordinated the efforts of German companies to produce all the materials necessary to supply German forces. Britain and France had far fewer factories and little heavy industry, and thus they were less prepared to produce the guns, shells, and heavy machinery vital to the war effort. Their governments also exercised less direct control over the people, making the coordination of production less efficient than in Germany. The Allied countries, however, had free access to the seas and were able to import many of their war materials from overseas, especially from the United States.

As the war progressed, Germany, Great Britain, and France all succeeded at reshaping their economies to produce goods for the war. Factories making luxury goods or nonessen-

tials were either converted to war production or shut down; workers were shifted to new jobs; and whole industries—wine making in France and chocolate production in Germany—went into decline. But this did not mean that economic reorganization was easy. With so many men being called away to fight in the war—especially in France and Germany, where conscription was universal—labor was scarce. Workers in factories were forced to work long hours at jobs they had not chosen. Pay was often low, and as the war continued, food grew scarce. Under these difficult conditions, workers in many industries began to go on strike.

France faced its greatest labor unrest during 1917. During that difficult year, heavy losses at Verdun had brought military operations to a near standstill as troops refused to fight. The war-weariness extended to French civilian workers, many of whom were socialists (people who believe workers should own and control industry). According to John Williams, author of *The Other Battleground,* France saw a total of 689

Three French refugees return to their homeland and dig through the rubble.
Reproduced by permission of Archive Photos, Inc.

Interior of the Krupp cannon foundry in Essen, Germany. *Reproduced by permission of Archive Photos, Inc.*

strikes—affecting 293,000 workers— in 1917. The strikes and other labor unrest ended only when the popular Prime Minister Georges Clemenceau threatened to use force to send laborers back to work.

Germany, too, was plagued with unrest from its workers, who lived in conditions even worse than those endured by French workers. As the war ground on and the British blockade around Germany tightened, food grew increasingly scarce. Workers in Germany demanded higher pay and shorter hours, just like the French, but they also complained that they simply could not work without adequate food. In coal mines and steel factories, workers left their jobs. On April 16, 1917, some 220,000 workers staged nonviolent demonstrations in Berlin. They wanted more food, but they also called for an end to the war. Only the presence of army troops and the threat of imprisonment drove these workers back to their jobs. As if labor troubles weren't enough, the German economy was also increasingly challenged by the country's deteriorating system of roads and railways. Germany lacked the supplies and men to maintain the roads and railways, and it became more and more difficult to move goods and people throughout the country.

Shaping the Mind of a Nation: Propaganda

Wartime leaders realized that they would need the full support of the people to effectively wage war, and they set out to shape popular opinion in a variety of ways. Through propaganda—the spreading of ideas about the war that were favorable to the government—and through censorship—the suppression of war news that was unfavorable to the government—the French, British, and German governments tried to control how people viewed the war and the enemy.

Hate was the core of every propaganda campaign. The Germans, French, and British were all encouraged to hate those people who had once been their neighbors. It was not difficult to convince the French to hate the Germans. Many still remembered their galling defeat by the Germans in the Franco-Prussian War in 1871. The British were less inclined to such feelings, for Germany had long been one of their primary trading partners. In both France and Great Britain, however, stories of German atrocities soon encouraged people to think of the Germans as inhuman brutes. Shocking tales of German behavior circulated in newspapers and by word of mouth. One story told of how German soldiers cut the breasts off a Belgian nurse and left her to die; other stories, reports Williams, told of "raping of nuns, impaling of babies on bayonets, [and] mutilation of Belgian girls."

Germany's efforts to stir up hatred of the enemy were far more pervasive and systematic. Hatred of both France and Great Britain was encouraged by officials and preached in churches, but special emphasis was placed on hating Great Britain, which had blockaded German ports and was seen as the biggest obstacle to German victory. People were banned from speaking English; businesses and streets bearing English names received quick name changes to German. People throughout the country sang a "Hymn of Hate" against England, which concluded "We love as one, we hate as one, we have one foe and one alone—ENGLAND," according to Williams.

The ruins of the northeast wing of Chelsea Hospital, bombed by a German Air Force zeppelin. *Reproduced by permission of Archive Photos, Inc.*

Official censorship was also a powerful tool for shaping public opinion. In both France and Germany the newspapers were under the direct control of the military. War departments submitted their version of how the war was going, and newspaper editors were expected to print that news exactly as it was given to them. Even British newspapers, which had prided themselves on their independence, were forced to get most of their news from the government press bureau. They were reluctant to publish news that was unfavorable to the government for fear that they would be prosecuted under the Defense of the Realm Act (DORA), which gave the government broad powers to limit free expression. The result of this direct and indirect control of the news was that people within the combatant countries rarely received accurate reports about the war. Victories were exaggerated, and defeats were downplayed. When French soldiers mutinied in the summer of 1917, news of the trouble never even reached French civilians. In the end, the lack of accurate news may have been the only thing that kept citizens in both France and Germany from rising up in revolt.

The ultimate collapse of German popular support for the war was caused in part by successful British propaganda of another sort. Under the guidance of the Director of Propaganda in Enemy Countries, British writers

Poster for U.S. government bonds. *Reproduced by permission of Corbis Corporation (Bellevue).*

prepared leaflets in German that offered news of Allied victories and boasted of the huge numbers of American troops entering the war. These leaflets were attached to balloons and floated eastward into Germany. "By October," writes Williams, "167,000 a day were being released over the enemy lines." When the balloons popped, the leaflets floated downward, reaching retreating German troops and war-weary civilians. One German general complained that this "paper war" was ruining the morale of his soldiers. Even General Paul von Hindenburg, the supreme commander of the German army, lamented that "the enemy has taken up arms against German morale, seeking to poison it," according to Williams.

Hardships: The Battle for Food and Warmth

Of all the battles being waged on the home front, the battle to obtain adequate food and heating fuel (coal and wood) was by far the most important to civilians. The food and fuel situation in each country was quite different, but in every country it had a great influence on the people's will to work and bear the difficulties of war. France fared the best of any nation: Its agricultural system was well developed before the war, and France was capable of growing and producing much of its own food.

Through 1916 the British had not experienced many shortages of food, and they were cheered by reports that their naval blockade was pushing the German people close to starvation. Prices were rising, to be sure, but meat and bread were still widely available. All this was to change with the intensification of German submarine warfare in the spring of 1917. Germany intended to use stepped-up submarine attacks—on Allied merchant ships carrying food and other supplies— to show the British what it was like to go hungry. By the middle of 1917 the British government began calling for voluntary rationing of food. The government established guidelines for meat, potato, and bread consumption, and limited the availability of sugar. In addition, the government began the "allotment system," which set aside unused land of all sorts for small gardens. Across the country, people began planting vegetables to supplement their diets; even the king and queen tended a small garden near their palace. By 1918, however, these voluntary measures were no longer enough to ensure adequate food, and the government demanded mandatory rationing of most foods. Citizens were given a card that allowed them to purchase certain amounts of key items; once the card was punched, no more food could be purchased until the next card was issued. Rationing conserved limited food supplies, but it was disastrous for morale. Luckily for the British, the war was almost over.

While France and Britain experienced occasional food shortages, German citizens suffered a diminished food supply almost from the outset of the war. With a cooler climate and a smaller agricultural system, Germany couldn't produce enough food for itself. With the British blockade of German seaports, Germany's ability to import food was severely limited. The rationing of bread in Germany began in January 1915, just five months after the war began. The government issued a document called the *Ten Food Commandments,* which offered guidelines for conserving food, but as shortages continued, mere guidelines would not be enough. The War Food

Child in a refugee camp in Salonika, Greece.
Reproduced by permission of Archive Photos, Inc.

Office, established in 1916, created more than 250 rules for rationing almost all food items. Its leader, a man known as the "Food Dictator," was determined that all Germans should share in the deprivation. However, wealthier Germans were usually able to buy food illegally.

As the British blockade tightened, Germany's food miseries increased. Workers had so little food that they lacked the energy to work long hours; many went on strike not for higher wages, but for bigger food rations. Mothers sacrificed their own limited food supplies so their children could eat. Some people ground nuts and beans to stretch the flour for their bread; others ate horse meat, rats, and hamsters to try to get some protein; and farmers killed their precious milk cows for their meat. The winter of 1916–17 was known as the "turnip winter," because Germans took to eating the root vegetable that had only been used to feed livestock before. And, as elsewhere, matters got even worse in 1918. Throughout the country, people grew thin, haggard, and listless; doctors worried about the health of children. People rioted in the streets for food, and normally law-abiding Germans took to stealing food to avoid starvation. In this situation, Germany's surrender in November 1918 was a relief for the ordinary citizen. The terms of surrender could be no worse than what had already been endured.

Changing Role of Women

One of the biggest social changes of the war involved the expanded role women played in society. Before the war few women worked outside the home, except as domestic servants, and women did not have the right to vote. But during the war the need for laborers in war industries drew huge numbers of women into the workforce. Their great contribution helped prove a point that women had been arguing for years: Women were important contributors to the economy and ought to have the right to vote. In England and in the United States, women achieved the right to vote soon after war's end.

Women's participation in the war effort was at its greatest in Germany. In part this reflected the planning of the German government, which organized women to perform war-related work; it was also a necessity, for a high proportion of Germany's able-bodied men were serving at the front. In Germany, women worked in nearly every kind of job: They labored in factories, drove trams (streetcars), built roads, worked in mines, and performed tasks that have traditionally been assigned to women, such as cooking and making clothes. Without the contributions of Germany's women, the country's economy would have collapsed far sooner than 1918.

In Britain women were not directed into jobs as they were in Germany, nor did they work so openly in jobs that had

Women operating machinery in a munitions factory. *Reproduced by permission of Corbis Corporation (Bellevue).*

traditionally belonged to men. However, British women did volunteer in huge numbers to assist the war effort. When the government called for female volunteers in 1915, 124,000 women immediately came forward and were put to work in government posts, clothing trades, agriculture, and other areas. As many as 400,000 working-class women who had served as domestic servants left those jobs and found jobs that aided in the war effort; many never returned to their previous jobs, for they had tasted the pleasures of a higher wage at a more dignified job. British women had been outspoken in their calls for voting rights before the war, and their important contributions during wartime paid off in 1918 when Parliament granted them the right to vote.

In France women in agricultural areas took over the harvesting as soon as men went off to war in the fall of 1914, and women operated farms for the duration of the war. In the cities French women helped staff the munitions factories and served as nurses. By late 1915 there were some seventy-five

Women making Browning machine guns, working in the polishing shop, at Winchester Repeating Arms Company.
Reproduced courtesy of the Library of Congress.

thousand French women working in state-run factories. French women, too, enjoyed the newfound independence of working outside the home. In every country, the entrance of women into the workforce gave women a sense of independence and power that few had ever known. This experience transformed the way that many women saw marriage, and it contributed greatly to the modernization of gender roles that swept the Western world in the 1920s and 1930s.

1918: The Home Front in the Final Year

If the earlier years of World War I were a course in enduring the difficulties of total war, then the year 1918 was the final exam. Every effort the countries had made to rally around the war effort was intensified in the last year of war: Economic organization had to become more efficient, governments struggled to keep their people loyal, and citizens had to endure even greater hardships than they had known before. In

Terror from the Skies: Zeppelin Raids and Long-Range Artillery

As if enduring food shortages and long working hours was not enough, people in Great Britain and France were also subject to Germany's first attacks on civilian populations. One of the true "innovations" of World War I was the aerial bombing of civilian populations by German zeppelins. Zeppelins were giant cylindrical balloons filled with hydrogen. Powered by engines mounted underneath their giant bodies, these aircraft could fly over fifty miles an hour—and they could carry bombs. The Germans sent zeppelins across the English Channel to drop bombs on two coastal towns early in the war. The results were so successful that Germany increased the bombing dramatically in 1916, its zeppelins making 126 flights in all.

As part of the final German offensive in the spring of 1918, German forces unleashed a powerful new weapon that could catapult bombs long distances. From positions in the forests near Laon, about seventy miles from the city of Paris, German gunners fired the most powerful piece of artillery ever used in warfare. In eighteen days of bombing, the Germans lobbed nearly four hundred shells toward the capital city, killing 256 and wounding 625 people. In the worst single incident, a shell landed on a church full of worshippers on Good Friday, killing 88 people. The zeppelins and the long-distance shelling brought to civilians the fear and sudden death that was once experienced only by frontline soldiers.

this climactic year the French and British people proved capable of rising to the challenge, while the Germans were finally pushed beyond their limit by hunger and sheer exhaustion. When Germany surrendered in the fall of 1918, it was not just its army but also its people who were defeated.

France and Great Britain entered 1918 with two crucial advantages. First, they had not yet stretched their people to their capacity: More women could be brought into war industries if necessary, and food and fuel, while scarce, were still available—no one was starving. Second, the Allies knew that if they could hold out until the summer, they would be joined by fresh troops from the United States. Despite the fact that the German army had dramatic advances in the spring of 1918 and were closer to Paris than they had been since 1914, the Allies never gave up hope.

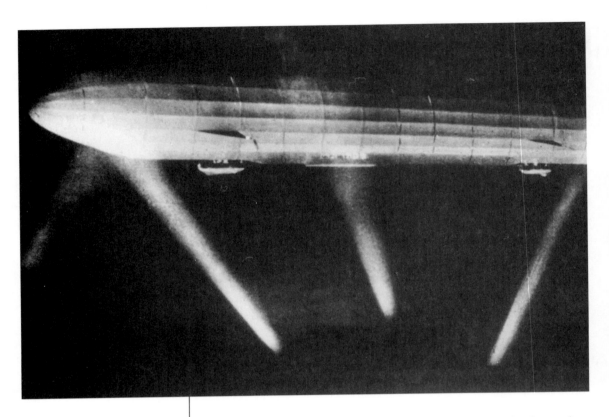

A German zeppelin caught in the searchlights during a bombing raid. *Reproduced by permission of Archive Photos, Inc.*

Germany entered 1918 knowing that it had one last chance to win the war. Germany's attacks on British shipping had failed to starve the British out of the war, and the growing presence of American troops in France meant that the Germans would soon have to face a fresh, well-supplied enemy. Worse, German civilians were starving, workers were threatening to walk off their jobs if the war did not end soon, and the civil government was faltering in its support for the war. Thus the Germans staked their chance at winning the war on one last offensive, launched in March of 1918. Across Germany, soldiers and civilians knew that this was their last chance. When the German offensive stalled in Augustand the Allies—now aided by American forces—began pushing back, everyone in Germany knew that the war was over.

Between August and November1918, the German war effort collapsed. The army fell back in retreat; the German navy, ordered to put to sea to avoid capture by the Allies, rose up in revolt against its officers. By October people in Berlin,

Spanish Flu: Death Hits the Home Front

In midsummer 1918, just as the Allies were beginning their final offensive that would drive the Germans to surrender, people across Europe began to die of a mysterious disease. Healthy people suddenly took to their beds, and within a short time many of them were dead. In Britain as many as 4,000 died each week; in Paris alone, the disease killed as many as 1,200 people a week. Superstitious people believed that this sudden outbreak of disease was divine revenge on a world embroiled in war, but in fact it was a deadly virus known as the Spanish Flu.

The Spanish Flu, which raged from mid-1918 through early 1919, killed 166,000 in France, 225,339 in Germany, and 228,900 in Great Britain. Overseas the death toll was even higher: In the United States 550,000 died; as many as 7 million died in India; and it is estimated that the flu killed one quarter of the population of the residents of the Pacific Islands. In all, the flu killed 20 million people around the world. No one has ever been able to explain why this strain of flu was so deadly or why it spread so widely. Since that time, scientists have developed vaccines to counter the worst strains of the flu and now feel confident that any future flu outbreaks can be contained more quickly.

Germany's capital, marched and protested for peace. Finally the kaiser (the German emperor) abdicated and fled to Holland; the government collapsed and a new, pro-peace chancellor took office. The people of Germany celebrated their "victory," for one of the first acts of this new government was to surrender and make peace with the Allies. The German surrender, announced on November 11, 1918, brought peace to a people desperate for an end to their suffering.

For More Information

"The First World War: The Home Front." [Online] http://www.sackville. w-sussex.sch.uk/FWWhome.htm. (accessed December 2000.)

"The Great War and the Shaping of the Twentieth Century." [Online] http://www.pbs.org/greatwar. (accessed October 2000.)

"The 1918 Influenza." [Online] http://www.library.utoronto.ca/spanishflu/1918.html. (accessed December 2000.)

"World War I: Trenches on the Web." [Online] http://www.worldwar1.com. (accessed October 2000.)

Sources

Dooly, William G. Jr. *Great Weapons of World War I.* New York: Bonanza Books, 1969.

Heyman, Neil M. *World War I.* Westport, CT: Greenwood Press, 1997.

Williams, John. *The Other Battleground: The Home Fronts: Britain, France, and Germany, 1914–1918.* Chicago: Henry Regnery, 1972.

Winter, J. M. *The Experience of World War I.* New York: Oxford University Press, 1989.

Winter, Jay, and Blain Baggett. *The Great War and the Shaping of the 20th Century.* New York: Penguin Studio, 1996.

Reluctant Warriors: The United States in World War I

10

For the United States, World War I was a short war. The United States did not join the Allies in their war against the Central Powers until April 6, 1917, thirty-two months after the war began, and U.S. troops did not see action until well into 1918. Then, just a few months after America's active entry into the war, the war was over. Though U.S. participation in the war was brief, it was vitally important. The United States tipped the balance of the war in the Allies' favor and brought the long struggle to an end. The agony of committing to a European war, the difficulties of managing mobilization and shaping public opinion, and the anguished debate about signing the Treaty of Versailles (the document that officially ended the war and re-established peace in Europe) were crucial moments in American history.

Watching the War from Afar

When war broke out in Europe in August 1914, Americans watched with a combination of dismay and relief. Many Americans had deep cultural ties with the major combatant nations, and it was difficult to watch those nations enter into a costly and terribly bloody war. Like the rest of the world, the United States had been enjoying a time of great peace and prosperity, and the war upset these tranquil times. Yet because of its great distance from the conflict and its history of noninterference in European affairs, the United States did not feel compelled to get involved in this war. The U.S. government was content to let Europeans fight among themselves. President Woodrow Wilson urged Americans to remain neutral in thought and deed.

Americans noted with pride the national characteristics that helped them avoid war. America's politicians congratulated themselves on avoiding the kinds of secret treaties and dangerous alliances that had drawn European nations into war. They boasted that U.S. interests lay in maintaining the strength of the domestic economy and not in bullying neighbors or fighting for distant colonies. Moreover, they blamed the European conflict on the combatants' inadequate commitment to democracy. Democratic countries responded to the will of their people, boasted the United States, and the people did not want war. Though some of these claims aroused skepticism both at home and abroad, many people firmly believed them.

The Difficulties of Neutrality

Strict neutrality would prove a difficult course to follow in the years to come. Officially, the United States remained neutral; it was willing to trade with the Allies and with the Central Powers, and it did not commit armed forces to either side. U.S. politicians carefully maintained their neutral stance up until the point of declaring war. Unofficially, however, the United States favored the Allies. The United States had close cultural and economic ties to the Allies, especially Great Britain. Both the flow of trade and the tide of public opinion strongly favored the Allies as the war went on. Thus, in the years between the beginning of the war and the U.S. entrance into it, the United States was neutral in policy but not always in practice.

The most direct and pressing link between the United States and the Allies was trade. American policy stated that the

United States would trade equally with all combatant countries, but the combatant countries certainly did not have equal access to American markets. With its tight blockade over German ports, Britain established virtually complete control of the seas early in the war. Thus only the Allies, with their highly developed shipping industries, had access to the American market. German ships simply could not escape the British blockade. But Germany soon discovered a weapon that could.

Submarines: Early Menace to Neutrality

The Germans were not willing to sit idly by while the Allies traded freely with the United States. Defying international agreements about how warships were to treat unarmed merchant ships (those that carried nonmilitary supplies), Germany launched submarine attacks on Allied shipping beginning in 1915. Such attacks were legal as long as the submarines surfaced, announced their intention to sink the ships, and provided for the survival of the ships' occupants. The German subs obeyed no such rules. Instead they engaged in unrestricted submarine warfare: Hidden under the sea, they launched torpedoes that sank ships and often killed all aboard. On March 28, 1915, a U.S. citizen was killed when the British liner *Falaba* was torpedoed by a German U-boat. Six weeks later, on May 7, 1915, 128 Americans were among the 1,200 people killed when a German sub sank the British liner *Lusitania*. To American politicians, German submarine warfare had become a crisis.

The United States protested the sinking of the *Lusitania,* and some in President Wilson's administration feared that the U.S. protests would lead the nation into war against Germany. After an exchange of diplomatic notes—interrupted by the killing of two more Americans by German subs—Germany

"Shall we be more tender with our **dollars** than with the **Lives of our sons**"

mcadoo
Secretary of the Treasury

Buy a United States Government Bond of the

2nd **LIBERTY LOAN**
of 1917

An Uncle Sam poster calling for support of the American war effort.
Reproduced courtesy of the Library of Congress.

slowed down its attacks. After further American pressure, the Germans issued the *Sussex* pledge on May 4, 1916. They promised not to sink merchant ships without warning and safety provisions. This pledge pleased German political leaders, who did not want America to join the war on the Allies' side, but it angered German military leaders, who hated to give up one of their most powerful weapons. Before too long, however, the Germans would return to unrestricted submarine warfare in a desperate bid to win the war.

Reluctant Warriors: The United States Enters the War

One thing was clear about American policy before 1917: The United States did not want to join the war. President Woodrow Wilson was strongly opposed to war as a means to solving international problems. He believed in diplomacy and thought that war was tremendously disruptive to the smooth flow of trade that would most benefit all nations. The American economy was running smoothly, not least because it had become a major supplier of goods and capital for the Allied war effort. Though Americans tended to sympathize with Allied war claims, the majority of the American people did not want war either. To them, the war was a European issue. Wilson was reelected to the presidency in 1916 partly because he campaigned on a platform of keeping the United States out of the war. But events soon led the nation into the war it had hoped to avoid.

In keeping with his reelection mandate, Wilson tried to get the warring sides to talk of peace in the winter of 1916–17. The Allies, however, refused to consider anything less than total victory. Realizing that they must fight to the finish, the Germans vowed to starve the British out of the war by again attacking any merchant ships that tried to bring food or other supplies to the Allies. The Germans announced this momentous decision on January 31, 1917, knowing that it would bring America into the war. Wilson, however, did not leap to declare war. He still wanted peace. In February, however, he learned of the so-called Zimmermann telegram, an offer from the Germans to the Mexican government that promised German support if Mexico would declare war on the

United States. Then in March German U-boats sank three American ships, the *City of Memphis, Illinois,* and *Vigilencia.* Pushed into a corner, Wilson appeared before Congress on April 2 to ask Congress for a declaration of war against Germany. Four days later, he officially took his country into a war that he said would "make the world safe for democracy." At last the Americans were in the war.

Preparing the Country for War

For nearly three years the government had counseled the American people to remain neutral. Suddenly, with the declaration of war on April 6, 1917, the American government placed its full weight behind a campaign to discredit the Central Powers, especially the Germans, and to prepare American industry and American soldiers to take their place in the war effort. Gone were neutrality and evenhandedness. With all the energy and determination for which it was known, America prepared itself for war. The results were not always pretty: Some wartime policies led to discrimination and repression, but they were seen as a necessary part of the war effort.

Among the first tasks facing the Wilson administration was the job of getting the American people solidly behind the war effort. In some ways this was not hard, for the American people responded with enthusiasm to Wilson's calls to crush the Central Powers. Yet there were many Americans who clung to their hope for peace or, because of their German heritage, sympathized with the Central Powers. For those who opposed the war effort, Woodrow Wilson had these words, as quoted in David Kennedy's *Over Here: The First World War and American Society:* "Woe be to the man or group of men that seeks to stand in our way."

The government launched a multifaceted effort to promote its war aims and crush domestic opposition. Even before the war, Wilson had spoken out about the dangers of so-called hyphenated Americans, Americans with close ties to their European countries of origin. Such people, Wilson told Congress in 1917, "have poured the poison of disloyalty into the very arteries of our national life. . . . Such creatures of passion, disloyalty, and anarchy must be crushed out. . . . [T]he hand of our power should close over them at once," as quoted in Kennedy. Because of this official stance of hostility, Americans of German, Austro-Hungarian, or Turkish descent soon found themselves subject to suspicion and open harassment. And that was just the beginning.

Repression and Propaganda

The Espionage Act, passed in June 1917, gave the U.S. government the power to suppress any opposition to the war. Under the authority of this law, Postmaster General Albert Burleson suspended the mailing privileges of prominent labor and socialist groups who promoted peace or threatened to go on strike in important war industries. Attorney General Thomas W. Gregory also was aggressive in hunting down anyone who publicly questioned the government's war efforts. He encouraged government attorneys to silence all dissent and openly praised mob actions against supposed anti-Americans. Gregory offered his praise to a band of civilian vigilantes known as the American Protective League. This group was 250,000 members strong, and according to Kennedy, its members "spied on neighbors, fellow workers, office-mates, and suspicious characters of any type. . . . Its 'agents' bugged, burglarized, slandered, and illegally arrested other Americans. They opened mail, intercepted telegrams . . . and were the chief commandos in a series of extralegal and often violent 'slacker raids' against supposed draft evaders in 1918."

Those treated worst by American "patriots" were German Americans. Once one of the most prosperous and well-liked immigrant groups in the United States, German Americans became the most despised. German Americans faced all varieties of hostility and discrimination, from slight social snubs to outright violence. In the worst case of anti-immigrant bias, a German American named Robert Prager was bound in an American flag and then brutally lynched (killed by a mob) in front of a cheering crowd of five hundred Americans in St. Louis, Missouri. His murderers were found not guilty by a jury; on returning the verdict, one jury member called out "Well, I guess nobody can say we aren't loyal now," according to Kennedy in *Over Here*. When the war began, a rumor circulated that the Germans were hatching a plot to have African Americans rise up throughout the South. This attempt to cast blacks as anti-American did not work, however, for most blacks came out solidly in support of the war (see sidebar).

Other efforts to encourage Americans to support the war were not quite so heavy-handed. More in tune with Wilson's progressive political views was the government war information agency, called the Committee on Public Information, or CPI. Headed by reformer and journalist George Creel, the CPI devoted itself to educating the American people about the correct attitudes to bear toward the war. Creel organized a small army of seventy-five thousand "Four-Minute Men" to travel throughout the country giving speeches to stir up enthusiasm for the war. The CPI encouraged the formation of "Loyalty Leagues" in ethnic communities and provided a wealth of information to teachers at every level of the American education system. However, according to Kennedy, the CPI soon transformed from a pure information agency to a "crude propaganda mill. The Committee began to place illustrated advertisements in mass magazines like the *Saturday*

Evening Post, exhorting readers to report to the Justice Department 'the man who spreads pessimistic stories . . . , cries for peace, or belittles our efforts to win the war.'" The CPI also resorted to spreading inaccurate stories of German atrocities and actively tried to stir up hatred of Germans.

American Industry

The war in Europe had been good for American industry and banking. American companies sold guns, shells, and other war materials; American farmers shipped massive amounts of food overseas; and American bankers were happy to loan money to grateful foreign governments. As soon as the United States entered the war on the side of the Allies, American industry joined with the government in gearing up for war. But it did so in ways quite unlike those of the other warring countries. In Germany, France, and to a lesser extent Great Britain, governments had taken charge of the nation's industries and openly directed how they would operate. In the United States, where businessmen's rights to independence were nearly sacred, the government acted more as a coordinator, encouraging cooperation and standardization in an effort to make industry work most efficiently. This cooperative relationship between business and government proved efficient and long-lasting.

Future president Herbert Hoover's management of the Food Administration offers a good example of how the U.S. government worked with American business. Hoover did not want to dictate to American farmers or food distributors what they should grow or what price they should ask for their products. But he did want to make sure that farmers would contribute the farm goods that were most needed, and that distributors would not charge excessively high prices. To reach his goals Hoover had the government offer high prices to encourage production, and he appealed to distributors' patriotism to encourage them to avoid excessive profits. Hoover believed that the government should serve industry in such a way as to make industry profitable and efficient, and he developed many ways to encourage such efficiency. Under his able guidance, American agriculture thrived during the war, and Americans never had to endure the rationing of food that most European countries suffered through. Many other American

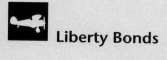

Liberty Bonds

One of the biggest problems facing the American government when it entered the war was how to raise the massive amounts of money it would need to build and supply the U.S. Army, not to mention the funds for direct aid to the Allies. Some politicians wanted to raise taxes, but the Wilson administration did not want to force Americans to bear the costs of the war so directly. Wilson wanted Americans to support the war voluntarily, and Secretary of the Treasury William Gibbs McAdoo proposed an incredibly effective plan: Liberty Bonds. Liberty Bonds were government-backed bonds that paid 3.5 percent interest (later raised to 4 percent). By purchasing these bonds people loaned the government their money, knowing that it would be repaid after the war was over. Because the bonds were sold in small denominations, even people with small incomes could purchase them.

Liberty Bonds were presented to the American people as an important way of supporting their country and showing their patriotism. McAdoo launched a massive publicity campaign to promote the bonds: Posters promoting bond sales appeared throughout the country; movie stars and popular writers gave speeches in support of the bonds; and Boy Scouts were authorized to sell them door-to-door. McAdoo made the importance of bond buying clear in a speech quoted by David M. Kennedy, author of *Over Here:* "Every person who refuses to subscribe or who takes the attitude of let the other fellow do it, is a friend of Germany and I would like nothing better than to tell it to him to his face. A man who can't lend his government $1.25 per week at the rate of 4% interest is not entitled to be an American citizen." It is not surprising that the government raised all the money it wanted with such propaganda campaigns.

industries worked with the government in a similar way and continued to do so after the war as well. The war taught America important lessons about how American business and government could work together.

Preparing the Soldiers

When Great Britain and France heard that the Americans were joining the war effort on their side, a great cheer went up in both countries. People there were happy that Amer-

African American soldiers returning home from Europe after World War I, wearing the *Croix de Guerre* medal given by the French government. *Reproduced by permission of Archive Photos, Inc.*

ican soldiers would soon be joining them in the front lines. No such cheer arose in America. Few Americans had considered the idea of creating a large American army, much less the idea of sending it to fight overseas. They expected that perhaps the American navy would help the Allies, or that American economic aid to the Allies would simply grow more substantial. Over the objections of many in the U.S. Senate and contrary to the long-standing American tradition of maintaining a small, volunteer army, Wilson asked for and received a large military budget and an army raised by conscription, another word for a draft of able-bodied male citizens.

In May 1917, the Selective Service Administration began registering for the draft all men between the ages of twenty-one and thirty. The first men were selected on July 20 and began appearing in training camps in September. They trained throughout the fall and began to cross the Atlantic toward France late in 1917. By the end of 1917, however, only 175,000 American soldiers had reached Europe, hardly enough to turn the tide for the Allies. The draft picked up speed early in 1918. All told, nearly a million American troops arrived in France in May, June, and July of 1918. It was clear that they were sorely needed. The Italians had experienced a disaster in the fall of 1917, the Russians had left the war, and the Germans had mounted a last, desperate offensive in March of 1918.

Americans in Action

In 1918, as the Germans' spring offensive pushed French and British troops backward all across the Western Front, Allied commander General Ferdinand Foch of France begged American general John "Black Jack" Pershing to allow American soldiers to serve in support of the French and British. Pershing, however, would not be budged. He was determined to retain control of American troops, even if that meant setbacks for his allies. The French and British withstood the German advance, and by August of 1918 the Americans, now thoroughly trained and at full strength, were ready to join in a concentrated attack.

Pershing favored aggressive assaults with masses of soldiers, techniques he had learned at the United States Military Academy (West Point). He quickly learned that that was not the way war was waged on the Western Front. In hard-fought and brutal battles in Saint-Mihiel, Belleau Wood, and the Meuse-Argonne Forest, American soldiers experienced intense machine-gun fire, artillery bombardments, poison gas—all the horrors of trench warfare. Fighting bravely they achieved success almost everywhere they fought, though they never broke into the open to gain the huge chunks of land Pershing desired. (For a more complete account of the battles the American soldiers participated in, see Chapter 4.)

Just a few months after American troops went into action, the war was over. The Germans had been reeling before the American troops arrived, but American input on the battlefield bowled them over. It wasn't just that the Americans fought well. What proved even more dispiriting to the German soldiers was how well supplied the Americans were. Near starvation and running out of bullets, the Germans knew that they could not continue to fight against an enemy so well fed and well armed. In the end, then, it was the presence of Amer-

African American Soldiers

African Americans were as eager as their white fellow citizens to support their country and help defeat the Central Powers. However, their involvement in the war effort was plagued by the same racial hatred and segregation that shaped civilian life. Military officials worried that white soldiers would not want to serve alongside blacks, so they agreed that black soldiers would serve in segregated regiments under white commanders. Blacks were first drafted in September of 1917 and were trained alongside white soldiers. By war's end, nearly 400,000 black soldiers joined the war effort.

White military leaders generally did not trust black soldiers in combat and assigned most of the black regiments to serve as laborers. Black troops were some of the first to arrive in France in the fall of 1917, and they set to work preparing the way for the troops still to come. They built docks, railways, and warehouses, and they unloaded the millions of pounds of war materials that the United States sent to France. It was not glamorous work, but it was essential to the success of the American war effort.

Two divisions of African American soldiers did see combat action in France. The Ninety-second Division, consisting entirely of draftees, served under American command. One regiment in the division performed poorly in its first battle, and the

ican soldiers as much as their fighting prowess that helped drive the Germans to surrender on November 11, 1918.

Failed Peace and America's Place in the Postwar World

In the years leading up to the war, U.S. president Woodrow Wilson had been the world's leading voice for peace. Even after the United States entered the war, Wilson sought ways to keep the Allies open to making peace. Early in 1918, Wilson gave a speech in which he outlined his hopes for a resolution of the conflict. In this address Wilson laid out the Fourteen Points, a blueprint for peace talks. When the Allies met to consider peace terms after the German surrender, the Fourteen whole division was removed from combat duty in shame. The Ninety-third Division, however, was a great success. Consisting of more-seasoned soldiers as well as some draftees, the Ninety-third served under French command. The French did not distrust blacks the way most American commanders did, and their commanders placed the black regiments in key positions during their battles. According to Michael L. Cooper, author of *Hell Fighters: African American Soldiers in World War I*, "The 370th [regiment] … captured nineteen hundred German prisoners in a single day. And both the 369th and the 372nd were awarded the Croix de Guerre [a French medal] for their effective fighting during the Meuse-Argonne offensive." The Ninety-third Division proved that black soldiers could fight as well as any white man.

Black leaders in the United States had hoped that blacks' participation in the war would lead to greater freedoms at home, but their hopes were cruelly dashed. Soldiers returned from France—where they had experienced real equality with the race-blind French citizens—to the same poor prospects they had left behind. Many of them could no longer endure life in the segregated South and joined in a great migration to plentiful factory jobs in the North. These black soldiers received little thanks at the time, but they are now recognized for their great contributions to the successful American war effort in France.

Points provided the basis for their discussion. (For a complete discussion of peacemaking, see Chapter 11: The Failed Peace.) Key to Wilson's vision of peace was the creation of the League of Nations, an international decision-making body that would help avoid future armed conflicts between nations.

Wilson's support of the League of Nations raised a political issue that had been buried when America united to fight the war: the problem of America's relationship with the rest of the world. Wilson and his political allies—called internationalists—believed that America's future prosperity would lie in global trade. They thought that America should protect its economic interests overseas by cooperating with other countries to avoid warfare and other disruptions of trade. Wilson's political foes—who dominated the Senate—were known as isolationists. They believed that the United States was better

President Woodrow Wilson is cheered by an enthusiastic crowd as he passes through the streets of San Francisco. *Reproduced by permission of Archive Photos, Inc.*

off avoiding entanglements with foreign countries and that America should concentrate on building up its domestic economy. The disagreement between these two groups over U.S. participation in the League of Nations was nothing less than a fight for the future of America.

American participation in the League of Nations was part of the Treaty of Versailles, the treaty that made peace between the Allies and Germany. Like all treaties affecting the United States, the Treaty of Versailles had to be approved by the Senate. Unluckily for Wilson and other internationalists, the leader of the isolationists in the Senate was Wilson's bitter political enemy, Republican senator Henry Cabot Lodge. Lodge phrased his objection to the treaty simply: Participation in the League of Nations would diminish American sovereignty by allowing other countries in the League to dictate foreign policy to the United States. In a speech to the Senate on August 12, 1919, quoted in Daniel M. Smith's *The Great Departure*, Lodge said, "I object in the strongest possible way to having the United States agree, directly or indirectly, to be controlled by a league which may at any time . . . be drawn in to deal with internal conflicts in other countries, no matter what those conflicts may be. . . . It must be made perfectly clear that no American soldiers . . . can ever be engaged in war or ordered anywhere except by the constitutional authorities of the United States." Lodge and the isolationists eventually defeated the treaty in a political battle that left Wilson's health and political future broken.

The United States did not join the League of Nations. In fact, following its brief involvement in international affairs during the war, it largely retreated from foreign involvement throughout the 1920s and 1930s. Under Republican presidents the domestic economy grew dramatically in the 1920s, thanks in large part to the boost that had just been provided by the war. Although the United States had developed the strongest economy in the world, its strength proved no match for the worldwide economic depression of the 1930s. As a result, America was virtually powerless to keep Europe from plunging headlong into the Second World War in 1939. Could American involvement in the League of Nations and in the international economy have prevented either the Great Depression or World War II? Historians have been arguing over this question for years. One thing is clear: The isolationism that America returned to after the end of World War I was killed forever by World War II. Today, America is intimately involved in international politics and trade, and it presides over a sustained peace between the major world nations. Many historians now believe that Woodrow Wilson was ahead of his time in predicting how America would interact with the world.

For More Information

Friedel, Frank. *Over There: The Story of America's First Great Overseas Crusade.* Philadelphia, PA: Temple University Press, 1990.

Gay, Kathlyn, and Martin Gay. *World War I.* New York: Twenty-First Century Books, 1995.

Heyman, Neil M. *World War I.* Westport, CT: Greenwood Press, 1997.

Little, Arthur W. *From Harlem to the Rhine: The Story of New York's Colored Volunteers.* New York: Haskell House, 1974.

Sources

Barbeau, Arthur E., and Florette Henri. *The Unknown Soldiers: African-American Troops in World War I*. New York: Da Capo Press, 1996.

Cooper, Michael L. *Hell Fighters: African American Soldiers in World War I*. New York: Lodestar Books, 1997.

Kennedy, David M. *Over Here: The First World War and American Society*. New York: Oxford University Press, 1980.

Smith, Daniel M. *The Great Departure: The United States and World War I, 1914–1920*. New York: McGraw-Hill, 1965.

The Failed Peace

11

On January 8, 1918, nine months after the United States entered World War I on the side of the Allies, American president Woodrow Wilson (1856–1924) stood before the U.S. Congress to deliver the "Fourteen Points Address." In this speech he outlined a plan that would end the war and provide the structure for a lasting world peace after the war. Though this plan was greeted with praise from many, it did not impress the leaders of the warring nations. The Germans rejected the Fourteen Points out of hand, for they still expected to win the war. The French ignored the Fourteen Points, for they were sure that they could gain more from their victory than Wilson's plan allowed. Even the British, who were otherwise allied most closely with the United States, had doubts about Wilson's grand plans for world peace. As the war moved to a conclusion during the summer and fall of 1918, Wilson's Fourteen Points helped guide each country's thinking about how the postwar world might look. But when the warring countries actually sat down to settle their differences, the results were far from what Wilson imagined. The treaties that finally ended World War I reflected all the bitterness and hatred that had started the war; in fact, these treaties would pave the way for another generation of conflict.

Wilson's Fourteen Points

Wilson and the United States were in a unique position to shape whatever peace might come from four long years of war. First, the United States held what it considered to be the moral high ground. The United States had steered away from a war that clearly did not serve the interests of the people of any country, and it had been critical of the failure of European leaders and diplomats to resolve issues peacefully. Second, the high costs of waging war had severely weakened the once powerful countries of France, Germany, and Great Britain, and revolution was tearing Russia apart. By 1918, the United States stood as the most powerful nation in the world. It was with these conditions in mind that Wilson offered the world his Fourteen Points.

Wilson's Fourteen Points can be grouped into several sections. The first five points proposed general rules governing the behavior of all warring parties. They called for "open covenants of peace, openly arrived at" (as a protection against secret treaties), freedoms of the seas, free trade among nations, smaller armies, and new negotiations on colonial holdings that respected the people in those colonies. Points six through thirteen proposed specific territorial adjustments, most of which were interpreted as punishments for members of the Central Powers. These points granted territory to France and Italy, granted autonomy (self-rule) to the peoples of the Austro-Hungarian Empire and the Ottoman Empire, and established an independent Poland. The fourteenth point—key to Wilson's view of the postwar world—demanded that "a general association of nations must be formed under specific covenants for the purpose of affording mutual guarantees of political independence and territorial integrity to great and small states alike." This point, which came to be seen as a call for the creation of the League of Nations, was the most radical of Wilson's proposals and was met with the most intense opposition in the United States.

Wilson's announcement of his Fourteen Points well before the end of the war may have strengthened Germany's resolve to fight on, for the German kaiser and his military leaders wanted nothing to do with this peace plan. But no amount of German resolve could withstand the collapse of every one of Germany's allies and the growing strength of the American

army in Europe. Germany surrendered to the Allied forces on November 11, 1918, despite the fact that the Germans still remained in control of territory in Belgium and France. Many in Germany felt that they had not actually been defeated but instead had agreed not to fight any longer. But it was Germany who had surrendered to the Allies, and thus it was the Allies who would get to dictate the terms of peace. The question was whether that peace would be made under Wilson's idealistic plan or under the punishing demands of leaders from France and Great Britain.

President Woodrow Wilson on a speaking tour to promote the League of Nations, 1919. *Reproduced by permission of Corbis Corporation (Bellevue).*

The Peace Conference

When the Peace Conference began in the spring of 1919, twenty-seven nations gathered to deliberate. The interests of the smaller countries were quickly decided, and the major issues were soon left to four men: President Woodrow Wilson of the United States; Prime Minister David Lloyd

David Lloyd George, Vittorio Orlando, Georges Clemenceau, and Woodrow Wilson at Versailles.
Reproduced courtesy of the Library of Congress.

George of Great Britain; Premier Georges Clemenceau of France; and Premier Vittorio Orlando of Italy. These four men alone would decide the fate of the postwar world.

It quickly became apparent that the four men had very different ideas for how the peace should be settled. Wilson had succeeded at setting the agenda with his Fourteen Points, but he alienated his fellow leaders with his superior attitude and unyielding air. Quoted in Jay Winter and Blain Baggett's *The Great War and the Shaping of the 20th Century,* Lloyd George said of Wilson, "I really think that at first the idealistic President regarded himself as a missionary whose function it was to rescue the poor European heathen from their age-long worship of false and fiery gods. He was apt to address us in that vein, beginning with a few simple and elementary truths about right being more important than might, and justice being more eternal than force." Clemenceau, quoted in Zachary Kent's *World War I,* raged, "How can I talk to a fellow who thinks himself the first man for two thousand years who has known any-

thing about peace on earth?" Wilson supplied the sweeping visions of peace that the newspapers loved to quote, and he clung to his lofty notion that eventually became the League of Nations. But it was Lloyd George and Clemenceau who were determined that their countries would benefit from the ordeal they had just suffered.

Clemenceau's demands were extensive and held great moral weight, for his country had suffered the deepest scars from the fighting, both in terms of the numbers dead and the damage inflicted on French property. France wanted the Alsace-Lorraine region back—it had been lost to Germany in 1871—and it wanted to strip Germany of the power to wage offensive war. France wanted Germany to pay for the war, in every meaning of that phrase. Italy's position was also straightforward. Italy had entered the war to gain territory from Austria-Hungary, and it expected that the Allies wold honor their early promises of land gains for Italy.

An American sailor and Red Cross nurse stand with British Tommies celebrating the signing of the Armistice. *Reproduced by permission of Corbis Corporation (Bellevue).*

A happy crowd of Parisians wave their hats and flags during a celebration of the end of World War I on Armistice Day.
Reproduced by permission of Archive Photos, Inc.

David Lloyd George had a mixed agenda. Political pressures required that Lloyd George ask Germany to pay a high price for its defeat. After all, the British, too, had paid dearly for the war, and Germany ought to be made to repay British losses. Yet Lloyd George knew that crippling the German economy would also damage Great Britain, for Germany had been Britain's second-largest trading partner before the war. Lloyd George also sought to protect his country's colonial interests and its control of the seas.

The Treaty of Versailles

As they began to debate the issues, the Allies could agree on little. Key elements of Wilson's Fourteen Points were dropped; reparations—the penalty that the losing countries must pay to the winners—could not be agreed upon; control of distant colonies was hotly contested. The negotiations dragged on. Wilson returned home to shore up support for his

"Stabbed in the Back": German Reactions to the Treaty of Versailles

Friedrich Ebert, who led the German government when Germany signed the Treaty of Versailles, had little to do with waging the war his country had lost. He had come to power only late in the war, as the kaiser abdicated his throne and military leaders stepped down in early November 1918. Ebert and his governing Social Democratic party had little choice about signing the treaty; Ebert's generals had told him that Germany could fight no more. But Germans looking for an explanation of their failure in World War I soon made this civilian government their scapegoat.

At war's end, German soldiers returned home—not with their heads bowed in defeat, but with pride. After all, many argued, the German army had not truly been defeated, for it had never allowed the enemy on German territory and still held enemy ground it had conquered. Chancellor Ebert fueled this belief when he saluted a parade of soldiers with these words, quoted in *Prelude to War:* "I salute you who return unvanquished from the field of battle." Thus when Ebert signed the humiliating

treaty, many in the army and throughout Germany believed that the German army had been betrayed—"stabbed in the back"—by Ebert's civilian government.

Ill feelings about meeting the high costs imposed by the Treaty of Versailles grew in the coming years. More and more Germans denied their responsibility for causing the war and supported politicians who wanted to return Germany to its former power. In his autobiography, *Mein Kampf,* former army soldier Adolf Hitler reflected on how anger about the treaty could be used to rouse the German people: "What a use could be made of the Treaty of Versailles. . . . How each of one of the points of that Treaty could be branded in the minds and hearts of the German people until sixty million men and women find their souls aflame with a feeling of rage and shame; and a torrent of fire bursts forth as from a furnace, and a will of steel is forged from it, with the common cry: 'We will have arms again!'" Adolf Hitler tapped into such feelings in Germany and rose to power in the 1930s as the head of the Nazi Party.

position, and other leaders also returned to their countries for a time. Finally, by May of 1919, five separate treaties were prepared. The most important of these treaties, the one with Germany, is known as the Treaty of Versailles.

The Allies presented the treaty to the Germans for their signature on May 7, 1919. The language of the treaty was difficult for the proud Germans to swallow, but one element of the treaty was especially troublesome. Article 231 declared that "Germany accepts the responsibility of Germany and her allies for causing all the loss and damage to which the Allied and Associated Governments and all their nationals have been subject as a consequence of the war imposed upon them by the aggression of Germany and her allies." In short, this article insisted that Germany accept all the blame and guilt for starting the war. The Germans refused to sign. Within days the Allies announced their plans to march their armies into Germany, and the German government gave in.

The treaty visited a string of humiliations on Germany. First, Germany was to be forced to pay the Allies for all the damages German forces had inflicted (payments were to be made over a period of thirty years). Germany was stripped of her foreign colonies, forbidden from keeping an army in the western part of her territory (the Rhineland), forbidden from joining in union with Austria, stripped of her rights to import any war materials, deprived of the right to buy or build submarines, and barred from having an air force. Finally, her delegates were forced to sign the treaty at a humiliating ceremony at the Hall of Mirrors in Versailles, France, on June 28, 1919.

Dealing with the Other Central Powers

Germany, of course, was not the only loser of World War I. The other Central Powers—Austria-Hungary, Turkey (also known as the Ottoman Empire), and Bulgaria—were also forced to pay for their part in the war in separate treaties signed in 1920. The Austro-Hungarian Empire had already paid the ultimate price when it broke apart during the waning days of the war. Despite the fact that the empire no longer existed, the separate states of Austria and Hungary were forced to pay war damages to the Allies. Austria ceded large chunks of territory to Italy, and the new nation of Yugoslavia was formed out of the southern remnants of the empire. (The several states of Yugoslavia, including Bosnia and Herzegovina, Croatia, and Serbia, eventually fragmented during the Balkan Wars of the late 1990s.) Poland and the new nation of Czechoslovakia also claimed portions of the previously proud empire. Bulgaria,

too, was split up, with portions of its territory parceled out to the Romanians, the Yugoslavs, and the Greeks.

The Ottoman Empire was similarly dismantled by the Treaty of Sèvres.

One of the most vexing issues following the war was how to handle distant colonies. The French and British wanted to simply claim the German colonies they had defeated in war, but Wilson and the leaders of smaller countries wanted to preserve the idea that these colonies were independent. The Allies thus agreed to assign the former German colonies to the League of Nations, which in turn allowed them to be governed under the mandate, or loose control, of individual countries. Britain gained a mandate over two former German colonies in Africa, which are known today as Tanzania and Namibia; France gained control in Cameroons. Later in the century, each of these African countries gained its independence.

Children in the street welcoming German soldiers returning home after the Armistice. *Reproduced by permission of Corbis Corporation (Bellevue).*

Woodrow Wilson: Loser of the Peace

Woodrow Wilson, architect of the Fourteen Points and the strongest proponent of the League of Nations, was singularly defeated by his role in the peacemaking process. When he announced his Fourteen Points plan, Wilson set the agenda for the Paris Peace Conference at the end of World War I. However, Wilson soon found himself forced to compromise on many major issues. He gave in on reparations, on control of the seas, and on setting national borders, but he was not willing to compromise on his plans for a League of Nations, an international ruling body that would help settle disputes between countries. Wilson dreamed that the League of Nations—which would later become the United Nations—could solve any remaining problems between countries.

Wilson's position as the president of a democratic country gave him great moral authority. But trying to navigate U.S. democracy soon led to his undoing. From the moment Wilson took his country into World War I, he had run into political opposition. A core group of primarily Republican senators known as isolationists did not want the United States involved in European wars. They resisted Wilson's Fourteen Points, and they were firmly opposed to American involvement in the League of Nations. Isolationists believed that getting involved in the League of Nations would strip American leaders of their ability to make decisions to protect U.S. interests.

Wilson was unable to sign the Treaty of Versailles in June of 1919 because the U.S. Senate had not yet approved the treaty. Determined to get it approved, the ailing Wilson set out on a whirlwind tour of the United States to build support for the treaty. He covered eight thousand miles in twenty-two days, but the trip ruined his health. He soon suffered a stroke and was virtually incapacitated for several months. The Senate voted down the Treaty of Versailles, Wilson's great hope for world peace, and kept the United States out of the League of Nations. It was not until July 1921 that Congress passed a simple resolution declaring that the war was over. By then the rest of the world had moved on.

A Failed Peace

The various treaties signed at the end of the war settled territorial issues and laid the blame for the war squarely on the heads of the Germans. But these treaties could not bring the one thing that Europeans desired most: lasting peace. In fact, many historians have argued that the peacemaking of 1919 provided the conditions that led to World War II. The redrawing of the map of eastern Europe placed hostile ethnic groups in close contact with each other, as in Yugoslavia, and placed ethnic Germans in foreign countries, as in Poland and Czechoslovakia. Economic collapse and political turmoil fed the rise of fascist dictator Benito Mussolini in Italy and fueled the revolution and the rise of communist dictators in Russia. Most troubling of all for world peace, the humiliating terms of the Treaty of Versailles and the Germans' postwar economic distress helped fuel the rise of Adolf Hitler and the Nazi Party in Germany. The same bitterness and distrust between countries that had fueled the start of World War I lay like a fog of poison gas across Europe. In 1939, the German army would burst through this cloud of gas and take Europe and the world back into the horror of war.

For More Information

Bosco, Peter. *World War I.* New York: Facts on File, 1991.

Clare, John D., ed. *First World War.* San Diego, CA: Harcourt Brace, 1995.

"The Great War and the Shaping of the Twentieth Century." [Online] http://www.pbs.org/greatwar. (accessed October 2000.)

Heyman, Neil M. *World War I.* Westport, CT: Greenwood Press, 1997.

Stewart, Gail. *World War One.* San Diego, CA: Lucent, 1991.

"World War I: Trenches on the Web." [Online] http://www.worldwar1.com. (accessed October 2000.)

Sources

Elson, Robert T., and the editors of Time-Life Books. *Prelude to War.* New York: Time-Life, 1976.

Gilbert, Martin. *The First World War: A Complete History.* New York: Henry Holt, 1994.

Kent, Zachary. *World War I: "The War to End Wars."* Hillsdale, NJ: Enslow, 1994.

Stokesbury, James L. *A Short History of World War I.* New York: William Morrow, 1981.

Winter, Jay, and Blain Baggett. *The Great War and the Shaping of the 20th Century.* New York: Penguin Studio, 1996.

12 | Conclusion: The Costs of War

No matter how they are measured, the costs of World War I were enormous. Undoubtedly, the most tragic and devastating of the losses caused by the war was the loss of life. Millions of soldiers died in battle, and countless civilians were killed by the side effects of the war: starvation, disease, or—in the case of the Armenians in Turkey—genocide. Even greater numbers of lives were disrupted. Millions of soldiers survived the war with grave injuries, and families across the world were ripped apart by the destruction of war. The monetary losses associated with the war were equally enormous. The combatant countries threw millions of dollars into the war effort, straining their economies during the war and for years thereafter.

Were the sacrifices in lives and money worth it? Was anything settled by this four-year killing contest? In the aftermath of the war, Europe was in worse shape than it was when the war began. Empires were shattered, governments fell, and violent and destructive regimes came to power in several of the combatant countries. Perhaps the only country to truly benefit from the war was the United States, which emerged as the world's greatest power. Almost every other combatant was

The Cost of War

Any reckoning of the costs of World War I must begin with a roll call of the dead and wounded. The Allies, who emerged victorious, saw more than 5,100,000 men die in battle or from wounds received in battle. The losing Central Powers lost more than 3,500,000 men. By country, the dead are as follows:

Germany	1,800,000	Australia	59,000
Russia	1,700,000	India	49,000
France	1,384,000	United States	48,000
Austria-Hungary	1,290,000	Serbia	45,000
Britain	743,000	Belgium	44,000
Italy	615,000	New Zealand	16,000
Romania	335,000	South Africa	8,000
Turkey	325,000	Portugal	7,000
Bulgaria	90,000	Greece	5,000
Canada	60,000	Montenegro	3,000

These numbers are from Martin Gilbert's The First World War.

drained nearly to destruction by the conflict. In the end, World War I settled nothing. It merely set the stage for a war that would surpass it in its measures of death and destruction—World War II.

A Lost Generation

The total number of dead soldiers—8,600,000 men, or more than 5,600 soldiers killed per day for the duration of the war—is the baseline from which all other assessments of the war's cost must begin. Multiply the number of soldiers dead by the number of lives these deaths touched—parents, family, friends—and the toll of war mounts even higher. In *War and*

A priest reading funeral mass over a trench filled with French casualties.
Reproduced courtesy of the Library of Congress.

Social Change in the Twentieth Century, historian Arthur Marwick estimates that the war produced 5 million widowed women, 9 million orphaned children, and 10 million refugees, people ripped from their homes by the war.

Besides the huge number of dead soldiers, there were other military loses. Armies counted the cost of waging war in terms of casualties—the total number of men killed, wounded, taken prisoner, or missing. All told, the Allied forces had a casualty rate of about 52 percent—22 million of the 42 million men sent to war. The Central Powers lost 15 million of the 23 million men they mobilized, a 65 percent casualty rate. Austria-Hungary had the highest casualty rate—90 percent—followed by Russia at 76 percent and France at 73 percent.

Modern weapons like machine guns, fragmenting artillery, and poison gas injured soldiers of every country and sent them back to their families shattered and often disfigured. Many men bore scars or carried chunks of shrapnel in their bodies, but could continue with their lives. They were the lucky ones. Some lost arms and legs and could not return to jobs. Many were wounded in the face, some so badly that their faces had to be reconstructed. In France these men were known as *gueules cassées,* men with broken faces. Other soldiers bore no physical wounds but were devastated by what they had seen in war. These shell-shocked men often received little sympathy from a public that did not yet understand the psychological effects of war.

Many referred to those killed or wounded in the First World War as a "lost generation," using the phrase made famous by American author Gertrude Stein. Many soldiers, of course, were lost in battle, but many other soldiers and civilians simply felt lost after the end of the war. All the truths about national honor and virtue seemed to have been destroyed by the war, and many writers and thinkers wondered how to make sense of the new, modern world. In his war novel *A Farewell to Arms,* American writer Ernest Hemingway expressed the sense that old truths had been destroyed. One of the main characters in the book, an American ambulance driver on the Italian front, reflects:

> I was always embarrassed by the words sacred, glorious, and sacrifice and the expression in vain. We had heard them, sometimes standing in the rain almost out of earshot, so that only the shouted words came through, and had read them, on proclamations that were slapped up by billposters over other proclamations, now for a long time, and I had seen nothing sacred, and the things that were glorious had no glory and the sacrifices were like the stockyards at Chicago if nothing was done with the meat except to bury it.

The Financial Toll

Because it is impossible to place a price tag on human life, calculating the total costs of the war is a difficult task. Several economists, however, have attempted a rough estimate. Shortly after the war, the Carnegie Endowment for International Peace estimated that the war cost the world over $337 billion; a later estimate, quoted by Niall Ferguson in *The Pity of War,* sets the cost at $208 billion. Whichever figure is closer, there is no doubt that the cost was staggering. These figures count the costs of productive lives lost, ships sunk, buildings and farms destroyed, and many other costs of war. The war had come at a time of unprecedented prosperity for Europe, and that prosperity and productive capacity were used to fuel a vast killing machine.

Memorial Day for soldiers buried at the war cemetery in Brookwood, Surrey.
Reproduced by permission of Archive Photos, Inc.

Once the killing stopped, Europe's economies did not return to their prewar expansion. Germany, of course, was devastated. Mass poverty among the working classes led to rapid inflation, and politicians could do little to stop it. Many of the country's profits went toward paying the reparations to the Allies. Throughout Europe, wages for most workers stayed low, while prices for food and other goods soared. Nations had borrowed heavily to finance their war efforts, and they spent years following the war struggling to repay their debts. Just as the political problems left at the end of World War I led inevitably to World War II, the economic troubles of European nations contributed to the worldwide economic depression of the 1930s.

The Unsettled Peace

Those who enter into a war usually do so believing that the war will settle things. Entering into World War I, Germany

wanted to establish itself as the supreme power in Central Europe; Austria-Hungary wanted to cement its influence in the Balkans; France and Britain wanted to control the power of Germany and ensure their shared (if not equal) dominance of Europe and distant colonies; Russia wanted to secure its influence in the Balkans and keep Germany's power under control; and the Ottoman Empire wanted to reestablish itself as the dominant power in the Middle East. The shape of the postwar

Europe after the Treaty of Versailles. *Reproduced by permission of The Gale Group.*

world reveals that not one of the major combatants achieved its goals. In the end, World War I settled nothing.

Unlike Germany and Austria-Hungary, Great Britain and France did not enter World War I with lofty goals of expanding their power. But as the victors in the war, they imposed a peace that created long-term problems. The biggest problem was their punishment of Germany. Moderates urged the Allies not to punish Germany too severely after the war, but rather to recognize that power needed to be shared among the major European countries (Great Britain, France, and Germany). However, politicians in Great Britain and France felt compelled to punish Germany. Their punishments humiliated the Germans and helped create the conditions that led to the rise of the Nazi Party, which came to power in part by promising to avenge the German loss in World War I. German politicians became obsessed with regaining Germany's position as a world power, and they started World War II to accomplish this goal.

The way the Allies imposed peace also caused other problems. First, they redrew the map of eastern Europe in ways that planted the seeds for future conflict. When they created the countries of Czechoslovakia and Poland, they gave these countries territory that Germany thought of as her own. After Germany regained power in the 1930s, these territories were the first prizes Germany seized in World War II. And the Allies' attempt to unite the southern Slavic peoples into a unified Yugoslavia brought together people with deep differences. These differences flared up throughout the century, leading to a brutal civil war in the 1990s. Second, Britain and France gained control of colonies in Africa and the Middle East, but many of these colonies were not content to remain under European control. In the Middle East especially, hostility to Western culture and Western control led to revolution and war. As the twentieth century progressed, Britain and France found it impossible to manage their colonial possessions. As with the peace they imposed on Germany, the peace they proposed for eastern Europe and for distant colonies created as many problems as it solved.

Revolution and Civil War in Russia

Russia was radically reshaped by its participation in the war. Russia got into the war in order to support its Serbian

allies in the Balkans, but its involvement in the war led to the Russian Revolution and a civil war that fundamentally reshaped the nation and the world. Participating in World War I so stressed the Russian political and economic system that a radical group known as the Bolsheviks took power in November 1917. The Bolsheviks, led by Vladimir Lenin, drew Russia out of the war by making peace with Germany. But Russia's troubles had just begun.

The Bolshevik or Red armies were opposed by the White armies of counterrevolutionaries who wanted to preserve the old order. In organized battles and in guerrilla raids, the Reds and Whites fought a bitter civil war for control of the country. White and Red forces alike committed brutal atrocities, slaughtering rival bands and any civilians who supported the other side. In southern Russia the Whites directed a pogrom, or organized massacre, of approximately 100,000 Jews. The Red secret police executed thousands of people who would not support their cause. According to Robert T. Elson,

A truck carrying Russian revolutionaries in Petrograd (St. Petersburg), Russia.
Reproduced by permission of Archive Photos, Inc.

author of *Prelude to War,* "those five ghastly years of civil war, accompanied by the famine and pestilence, killed up to 15 million Russians—6.5 million more than the total deaths on all fronts during World War I."

By 1921 the Reds had secured power in Russia. The country was so devastated economically that Lenin announced strict government control over all areas of the economy. This New Economic Policy was the basis for communist control of the country; under this policy the government received all economic gain and distributed it to the people. Lenin—and later his successor, Joseph Stalin—brutally suppressed any resistance to communist rule. Stalin consolidated Russia and several independent republics into the Union of Soviet Socialist Republics (U.S.S.R. or Soviet Union). The U.S.S.R. grew into a world power in the years to come, and it promoted the spread of communism around the world. After World War II, the Soviet Union's power was contested following World War II by the leading capitalist countries, especially the United States, which believed in allowing individuals and businesses to improve themselves without much government intervention. The Cold War between these countries ended in 1989 with the collapse of the Soviet Union.

The Rise of Nazism in Germany

The moderate German government that had signed the Treaty of Versailles with the Allies found itself in an impossible position. Not only was it shackled with rebuilding a country under the difficult conditions imposed by the peace, but its political enemies accused the government of betraying the German people by surrendering. Rival political groups vied for power in postwar Germany. Socialists and Communists hoped that they might stir up a revolution among the workers like the one taking place in Russia. Right-wing groups—which included the upper middle class and the army—argued that Germany needed to return to a position of power. One small party, the German Workers' Party, seemed to promote both worker control and the return of German industrial might. A young former soldier named Adolf Hitler soon joined this party, renamed it the National Socialist German Workers' Party (shortened to Nazi Party in Germany), and set his sights on power.

As the leader of the Nazi Party, Hitler electrified listeners at party rallies with his call for a powerful, triumphant Germany. Over the years, Hitler and his Nazi Party slowly claimed ever greater power, allying themselves with the German military and stirring up racial hatred with their anti-Jewish propaganda. Hitler received enough backing from the German parliament to become chancellor in 1933, and he quickly acted to secure ultimate power. Within months he banished all other political parties and imprisoned his political enemies. By 1934 Hitler had secured the office of president as well. Hitler led his nation in rebuilding its military strength and began to plot Germany's rise to world power.

When the Allies and Germany signed the Treaty of Versailles on June 28, 1919, many observers feared that the treaty satisfied the Allies' desire to punish the Germans but did not provide for a lasting peace. According to James Stokesbury, author of *A Short History of World War I,* French marshal Ferdinand Foch, upon reading the peace treaty, cried out, "This isn't

The wooden propellers of Germany's air fleet being cut up for firewood after planes were destroyed under the terms of the Treaty of Versailles
Reproduced by permission of Archive Photos, Inc.

peace! This is a truce for twenty years!" Foch was right. Twenty years and sixty-seven days after signing the treaty, Germany launched the attacks that soon engulfed the world in World War II. Most historians lay the blame for World War II directly on the failed peace of World War I.

The End of Old Empires, the Beginning of New

The war brought changes to many other nations, though few of these changes were as dramatic as those in Germany and Russia. Italy, which felt cheated by its failure to gain more from its involvement in the war, soon fell under the spell of a political leader named Benito Mussolini. Mussolini was a fascist dictator, which meant that he held complete power in his country and brutally suppressed opposition. Mussolini became Hitler's great ally in the years leading up to and including World War II. Turkey also entered a period of political turmoil, which brought the downfall of the sultan (king) and the rise of republican leader Kemal Atatürk, the father of modern Turkey. The Austro-Hungarian Empire disappeared, broken up into Austria, Hungary, and pieces of several other nations.

The one country that emerged from World War I in decent shape was the United States. Compared to the other countries, the United States had taken very little loss of life, and by delaying its entry into the war until nearly the end, it had avoided the severe financial strains of waging war. Financially strong when others were weak, the United States became the world's most dominant nation during and after World War I. It developed an army and navy of which it could be proud. It provided aid of many sorts—money, food, supplies—to countries devastated by war. Furthermore, while most European economies struggled throughout the 1920s, the U.S. economy boomed, lifting the nation into a time of unprecedented prosperity. Despite the United States' strong position at the end of the war, many Americans were not yet ready to accept their country's role as the leader of the Free World. Isolationist senators refused to sign the Treaty of Versailles, and throughout the 1920s and 1930s the United States tried to stay out of European affairs. That isolation was finally ended when America was pulled into World War II.

A War without Winners

The Allies dictated the terms of peace to the vanquished Central Powers at the end of World War I. But it is difficult to say that the Allies won, for World War I was truly a war without winners. Every country involved was decimated by the extreme loss of life, and most countries continued to experience severe economic troubles years after the end of the war. The war also crushed the spirit of millions of people around the world. Many had hoped that the rising tide of industrialism and world trade would create a more prosperous, peaceful future. But World War I only proved that nations would use advances in industrial capacity and technology to sponsor widespread destruction and killing.

Romagne Cemetery in France, where more than 23,000 Americans are buried, after losing their lives at Saint-Mihiel and Verdun. *Reproduced courtesy of the Library of Congress.*

For More Information

Bosco, Peter. *World War I.* New York: Facts on File, 1991.

Clare, John D., ed. *First World War.* San Diego, CA: Harcourt Brace, 1995.

"The Great War and the Shaping of the 20th Century." [Online] http://www.pbs.org/greatwar. (accessed October 2000.)

Heyman, Neil M. *World War I*. Westport, CT: Greenwood Press, 1997.

Kent, Zachary. *World War I: "The War to End Wars."* Hillsdale, NJ: Enslow, 1994.

Stewart, Gail. *World War One*. San Diego, CA: Lucent, 1991.

"World War I: Trenches on the Web." [Online] http://www.worldwar1.com. (accessed October 2000.)

Sources

Elson, Robert T., and the editors of Time-Life Books. *Prelude to War*. New York: Time-Life, 1976.

Ferguson, Niall. *The Pity of War*. New York: Basic Books, 1999.

Gilbert, Martin. *The First World War: A Complete History*. New York: Henry Holt, 1994.

Hemingway, Ernest. *A Farewell to Arms*. New York: Charles Scribner's Sons, 1929, 1957.

Heyman, Neil M. *World War I*. Westport, CT: Greenwood Press, 1997.

Marwick, Arthur. *War and Social Change in the Twentieth Century: A Comparative Study of Britain, France, Germany, Russia, and the United States*. New York: St. Martin's Press, 1974.

Stokesbury, James L. *A Short History of World War I*. New York: William Morrow, 1981.

Winter, Jay, and Blain Baggett. *The Great War and the Shaping of the 20th Century*. New York: Penguin Studio, 1996.

Index

naval 113, 123–135 (ill.)
Passchendaele 63–65
race to the sea 40–41
Somme, the 49, 52–54, 79
spring offensive 67, 68–73
Tannenberg 88–90 (ill.), 94
Verdun 49–51
war zones during WWI
106 (ill.), 111 (ill.)
weather conditions affecting
63, 92–93, 108, 111, 113, 116
Ypres (First) 41
Ypres (Second) 45, 46
Ypres (Third) 63–65
Battleships. *See* Weapons:
battleships; Weapons:
dreadnoughts
BEF (British Expeditionary Force)
27, 30, 37–39, 43, 48
Belgium
allies of 9–10
casualties 42, 199
invasion of 24, 29, 32–35
Belleau Wood 181
Bethmann Hollweg 83
Bismarck Archipelago 107
Bismarck, Otto von 2, 3, 4 (ill.)
Black Hand, the 16, 17, 20, 21
Black soldiers. *See* African
Americans, treatment
and role of, during WWI
Blockade, naval 67, 123, 129,
151, 162–163, 173
Boer War 39
Bolsheviks 100, 101, 205
Bombing, ruins caused by 82 (ill.),
160 (ill.)
Bombs. *See* Airplanes: bombs
dropped by; Weapons:
bombs, mines, and explosives
Bonds, posters promoting
purchase of government
161 (ill.), 173 (ill.), 179
Bosnia-Herzegovina 13, 16,
20, 194
Brest-Litovsk 94
British Expeditionary Force (BEF)
27, 30, 37–39, 43, 48
Brusilov Offensive 96–97 (ill.)
Brusilov, Aleksey 96
Bulgaria 13
armistice signed by 82,
102–103
casualties 199

peace treaty terms regarding
194–195
strategic role of, in WWI 92
Burleson, Albert 176
Byng, Julian 62

C

Cabrinovic, Nedeljko 20
Cadorna, Luigi 120
Cambrai, Battle of 65, 146–147
Cameroons 107, 108, 195
Canada, role of, in WWI 62,
75, 199
Caporetto, Battle of 120
Carol I 97
Carolines, the 107
Carpathian Mountains 110 (ill.)
Casualties 33 (ill.), 60 (ill.),
200 (ill.)
casualty rates 200
deaths in combat 199
Caucasus Mountains 110
Cavalry used in WWI 28
Cemal Paśa, Ahmed 117
Cemeteries for WWI soldiers
202 (ill.), 209 (ill.)
Censorship 159, 160
Central Powers 1, 11, 105, 194
attack on Serbia by 92–93
casualty rate and soldiers killed
in combat 199, 200
collapse of 81–83
naval strategy of 123, 133–135.
See also War plans; Western
Front: strategy used on the
surrender of 103
Champagne, First Battle of 44
Champagne, Second Battle of 47
Charles I 101
Chemical warfare 46. *See also*
Poison gas
Chemin des Dames 71
Christmas Truce 42
Churchill, Winston 113
Civilian attitudes toward WWI
early in the war 12–13, 14, 24,
28–29
in Austria-Hungary 101
in Germany 161, 169
in Russia 93, 99
in the United States 171–172,
174, 176, 177

Flanders 42
Flu, Spanish 169
Foch, Ferdinand 69 (ill.), 73, 77,
    79, 181, 207–208
Fokker, Anthony 149
Fonck, Paul-René 149
Food shortages and rationing
    161–164, 178
Fort Douaumont 50, 51
Fort Vaux 50, 51
Fourteen Points, the 182–183,
    187, 188, 190, 192, 196
France
    alliances of 3, 5–6, 7, 24
    army revolt of French soldiers
        61–62, 157, 161
    casualty rate and soldiers killed
        in combat 52 (ill.), 199, 200
    colonies of 107, 204
    goals of, in WWI 203
    government of, prior to WWI
        5–6
    industry and manufacturing in
        7, 156–158
    military and naval strength of
        7, 9, 11
    population of 7
    soldiers (ill.) 35, 40, 52, 152
    war plans 26–27, 44, 45
Franco-Prussian War 3, 5, 159
Frantz, Joseph 148, 151
Franz Ferdinand 1, 15, 16–18,
    19, 91
Franz Josef I 4, 5 (ill.), 19, 22, 101
French, Sir John 37
Fuel for heat, shortage of, during
    WWI 161–162

G

Galicia 85, 90, 91, 100
Gallipoli 113–115, 122
Garros, Roland 148, 149–151
Gas attacks. *See* Poison gas
Gas masks 142 (ill.), 143
Genocide. *See* Armenian genocide
    111, 112, 198
George. *See* Lloyd George, David
German Americans, treatment of,
    during WWI 177
German East Africa 107, 108–109
German Empire 3
German New Guinea 107

German Southwest Africa 107, 108
German Workers' Party 206
Germany
    alliances of 3–5
    armistice signed by 83,
        193–194
    borders of, 1914 (ill.) 18
    casualties 199
    colonies of 106–109, 194, 195
    economy 8, 192, 197, 202
    first major attacks by 36 (ill.)
    goals of, in WWI 202–203
    industry and manufacturing
        in 3, 12, 156–159
    military strength of 3, 10,
        11, 12
    naval strength and strategy
        11, 123–129, 133–135
    population of 3
    punishment of, after
        WWI 204
    soldiers (ill.) 17, 38, 43,
        89, 195
    spring offensive launched by
        67, 68–73, 74 (ill.)
    Treaty of Versailles 193–194
    war plans 24–26 (Schlieffen
        plan), 44, 48, 68–69
Gorlice 93
Great Britain
    alliances of 7
    casualties 199
    colonies of 6, 107, 204
    economy of 6
    expeditionary force from 27,
        30, 37–39, 43, 48
    goals of, in WWI 203
    industry and manufacturing
        in 9, 156
    military and naval strength
        of 9, 10, 11
    navy 7, 11, 44, 113,
        123–124, 125
    population of 9
    soldiers (ill.) 191
    war plans of 27, 43–44
Great Depression, the 185, 202
Great War, the 1
Greece 13, 102
Gregory, Thomas W. 176
Guns. *See* Weapons: artillery;
        Weapons: machine guns
Guynemer, Georges-Marie 149

Q

Quénault, Louis 148, 151

R

Railway systems, importance of
12, 25, 28, 78, 92, 158–159
Rasputin, Grigory 93, 94 (ill.), 96,
98–99
Rathenau, Walther 156
Rationing of food during WWI
162–164, 178
Red Baron, the 149
Refugees produced by WWI
157 (ill.), 163 (ill.), 200
Reinsurance Treaty of 1887 3
Rennenkampf, Pavel 87, 88, 90
Reparations 192, 202
Revolution. *See* Russia:
revolution in
Richthofen, Manfred von (Red
Baron) 149
Rickenbacker, Eddie 149
Romania 97, 199
Romanian Front 110 (ill.)
Russia
alliances of 3, 5–6, 7, 24
army problems and revolt in
86, 99
casualty rate and soldiers killed
in combat 199, 200
communist control in 197, 206
economy of 8–9, 93, 97,
197, 206
goals of, in WWI 203
government of, prior to WWI 6
industry and manufacturing
in 12, 97
military and naval strength of
9, 11, 12
offensives 86–91, 100–101
population of 12, 97
revolution in 97, 99–101, 197,
204–206 (ill.)
royal family of 100 (ill.)

S

Saint-Mihiel 75, 77, 181
Salandra, Antonio 119
Salonika Front 102

Sambre River 37
Samoa 107
Samsonov, Aleksandr 87–89
Sarajevo 16, 21, 91
Scheer, Reinhard 131, 132
Schlieffen plan, the 24–26 (ill.),
32–33, 38, 39
Schlieffen, Alfred von 24, 32
Selective Service Administration
(U.S.) 180
Serbia 95 (ill.)
allies of 9–10
battles in 91–93
casualties 92, 199
conflict with Austria-Hungary
13, 16, 19–23, 91–92
postwar events in 194
Sèvres, Treaty of 195
Shipping, WWI effects on
merchant 133–135, 151,
162, 173. *See also*
Blockade, naval
Ships. *See* Weapons: battleships;
Weapons: dreadnoughts
Siegfried Zone 59
Social Democrats 83
Socialist groups 12, 83, 157,
176, 206
Soldiers
American (ill.) 33, 34, 191
British (ill.) 191
French (ill.) 35, 40, 52, 152
German (ill.) 17, 38, 43,
89, 195
Italian (ill.) 119
killed in WWI 199.
See also Casualties
leaving home (Germany)
(ill.) 17
Solomon Islands 107
Somme, Battle of the 49,
52–54, 79
Sophie (countess; wife of Franz
Ferdinand) 16–17
South Africa, Union of 108
Soviet Union 206
Spanish Flu 169
Spee, Maximilian von 125
Spring offensive 67, 68–73,
74 (ill.)
St. Petersburg 28
Stalin, Joseph 206
Stallupönen 87

V

W

Y

Z